Library Serials Standards: Development, Implementation, Impact

PROCEEDINGS OF THE THIRD ANNUAL SERIALS CONFERENCE

Library Serials Standards: Development, Implementation, Impact

PROCEEDINGS OF THE THIRD ANNUAL SERIALS CONFERENCE

Edited by Nancy Jean Melin

MECKLER PUBLISHING
520 Riverside Avenue, Westport, CT 06880

3 Henrietta Street, London WC2E 8LU, England

Library of Congress Cataloging in Publication Data

Serials Conference (3rd : 1983 : Arlington, Va.)
   Library serials standards.

   Bibliography: p.
   1. Serials control systems--Standards--Congresses.
2. Libraries--Standards--Congresses. I. Melin, Nancy Jean. II. Title
Z692.S5S479 1983   025.3'432'02854   84-3789
ISBN 0-88736-008-4

Printed and bound in the United States of America

CONTENTS

PREFACE

From Emerald City to Crystal City

When the Third Annual Serials Conference's theme was chosen in late 1982, a location had not yet been selected. The choice of Crystal City (Arlington, Virginia) was especially fortuitous because several parallels between librarians' quest for standards and the journey to Emerald City became evident.

Devotees of the movie "Wizard of Oz" will remember that Dorothy, a young girl from Kansas, found herself swept by a twister to Munchkin Land in the County of Oz. To return to her home, she was told, she had to travel to Emerald City and seek the assistance of the Wizard. On the journey she enlisted as friends and companions a Scarecrow, a Tin Man, and a Cowardly Lion, who themselves sought the Wizard's help. The Scarecrow wanted a brain, the Tin Man a heart, and the Lion, courage.

Like the characters in Frank Baum's fantasy, librarians came to Crystal City in search of a wizard—standards. Librarians believe standards are magical, that they can be used to address many vexatious problems. Some of the problems are consequences of the demand for resource sharing, networking, and reliance on externally developed systems such as those of the bibliographic utilities. Like the Scarecrow, librarians seek a brain—standards; like the Tin Man, they seek a heart—widely inter-related library operations; like the Lion, they seek courage—courage to conform to standards.

Like Dorothy, most wish to go home—to return to simpler days of library management. But Dorothy never really returned from Oz; instead, she woke in her bed in Kansas.

The conference papers address various library-related standards. Recurrent themes include the impact of standards on library operations, the development and application of performance and production standards, and librarians' role in the design and implementation of standards. The contributors are librarians, publishers, subscription agents, vendors, and members of the standards-making community.

Taken together the papers support a common theme: Though standards are often difficult to accept and expensive to implement, they are essential to uniform practice throughout the library and information science communities.

Nancy Jean Melin

AN IRREVERENT LOOK AT THE IMPACT OF STANDARDS ON LIBRARIES

By Norman D. Stevens

"Where there is a standard method of doing a thing which has been accepted and approved over a considerable period of time, it is safe to assume that it is *wrong*." [John Cotton Dana][1]

With the exception of John Cotton Dana, one of my few heroes, librarians have taken an uncritical, accepting, and reverent view of standards. Their professional literature tends to be descriptive of the standards process, supportive of the idea of standards, and generally critical only of what I regard as minor aspects of the issue. This paper offers a somewhat more critical, less reverent look at the impact of standards on libraries.

In his unsuccessful bid to keep the Labour party in power in the 1954 election, Walter Nash, then prime minister of New Zealand, used a simple rhetorical device in several of his speeches. He described (in glowing terms) an accomplishment of his party, especially one being challenged, and then asked the audience: "Is that good, or is that bad?" It was, he said, a simple evaluative measure he had learned at a tender age from his grandfather. It is by Nash's simple but effective standard that I propose to evaluate the impact—past, present, and future—of standards on libraries.

In broad terms, the answer to that question is not as simple as Nash's answer as to whether the accomplishments of the Labour party were good or bad. In a British seminar in 1967 on what has become a major element of the standards question—the organization and handling of bibliographic records by computer—Jolliffe, Line, and Robinson made this observation:

> The attitude of librarians to standardization of all kinds has been ambivalent. They have argued in their writings and speeches for uniform standards and practices, they have set up committees to design standard codes of cataloguing practice, and at the same time nearly every library is non-standard to a greater or lesser degree in many of its operations and records. This puts standardization into the category of good things that no-one seriously expects to attain and few really want, like sanctity.[2]

The authors, of course, went on to argue that such ambivalence is bad and that librarians should, as a profession, make a stronger commitment to the acceptance and implementation of standards.

No librarian opposes standards. I certainly do not. But I would argue that an ambivalent attitude may be good, not bad. Librarians need to handle their work and to advance, through the use of standards *where they are appropriate* and through other means *where* they *are appropriate*. Librarians need the ability to accept or reject standards. Even Jerrold Orne, for many years the most active proponent of library standards, pointed out that "if a standard does not work, is not accepted and used, it will not last. It can work only if it is developed out of the experience formed in actual application."[3]

Pragmatic, Evolutionary Approach to Standards

Much of librarians' ambivalence can be attributed to their adoption of a pragmatic and evolutionary approach to standards. Wigington and Wood, for example, suggest that

> a major characteristic of the development of ... a national information transfer network ... is that improvements are brought about by evolutionary change. Evolution in turn involves a succession of standards for each part of the system, and compatibility with the rest of the system is an essential requirement for any new part. When the investment in an existing system is very large, that system cannot be replaced or revolutionized very quickly; it must be changed gradually as the economic and human resources are available to do so. The standardization of what the system handles, and the procedures for doing it, must change with that evolution. The standardization must also be effected with great care both to gain sound current operations and to facilitate future change.[4]

And Swanson's remarks on the broad issues of national information policy and the need to develop large-scale systems from the bottom up through trial and error, though never specifically mentioning standards, apply to standards as well. I recommend his article "Evolution, Libraries, and National Information Policy."[5]

Standards, to be adopted and effective, must grow out of practical experience, must work, and must be accepted and used. Only then will they have an impact. The professional literature, and library work at "higher" levels, is replete with arguments, theoretical justifications, and comments on the development of standards, and other rigamarole of little practical value. Fortunately these arguments have been largely ignored by librarians and thus have had little impact. I believe the pragmatic approach of accepting only those standards that prove to be useful is the ideal way to run our railroad.

If anything, there now appears to be a very serious danger that librarians, overwhelmed by technology, are rushing headlong into the blind acceptance and use of standards. They are doing so without carefully thinking through the effect of those standards on the quality and cost of library services. Let us consider some insights on standards and their use, in hopes they will help us return to the more cautious and pragmatic approach to standards that characterized earlier times. Such an approach is still appropriate. Let us look briefly to the past, consider in greater detail the present, and contemplate a few unusual prospects for the future.

One final introductory note may be in order. Typically a paper of this kind might begin with some definition of "standards." With Schmierer, I choose to assume "answers to broad and general questions about standards (viz., What are standards? Who produces them? How are they produced?) to be matters of common and routine knowledge, requiring neither explanation nor elaboration."[6] I reject the notion that "standards are in fact only faintly understood, and their increasing importance in several spheres of librarianship and information science demands that answers to these and other questions become common and routine knowledge."[7]

Standards in the Past

One of the simplest and still most effective standards is the alphabetization of information. This simple approach to the organization of knowledge is the keystone of much library work. Librarians should be proud to realize that "it is a reasonable and attractive hypothesis that the principle [of alphabetic arrangement] was first put to effective use by the scholars of Alexandria in response to the problems they faced as a result of the accumulation under their supervision of such an unprecedented mountain of literature and information."[8]

Alphabetization is an example of a standard that developed out of practical need, was accepted and used, and has stood the test of time. (Librarians would be fortunate to have other standards as simple and enduring.) In fact, alphabetical arrangement may be *the* single standard that has had the greatest impact on libraries through the ages. And it is a standard that will continue to be important.

Alphabetization set the stage for subsequent efforts to organize information in a standardized way. In studying library history one notes a steady increase in various efforts (many of them cooperative) to promote the use of standards, largely as a means of achieving a prescribed level of uniformity and of evaluating performance.

For many years standardization was seen—as it properly should be—as a tool, not a solution. The few late nineteenth- and early twentieth-century commentaries on standardization seem, as does much of the library literature of that time, quaint by today's standards. Typical of their approach was a series of comments on the question, "What Does 'Standardization' Mean?" that appeared in *The Wilson Bulletin* in 1925. Arthur E. Bostwick, John Cotton Dana, Frank K. Walter, Ernest J. Reece, Asa Wynkoop, and Adeline B. Zachart examined the question. Bostwick may have put it best when he ventured that "it will be necessary to show before anyone will adopt ... [standards] in a specified case that something is actually gained by it."[9] Dana, as one might expect, was more outspoken. He felt that

> we need ideas, suggestions, criticism, and aids of any kind to new lines of work, and more useful activities. These new things can perhaps be found; but not readily unless we look for them. Instead of looking for them, and, when found, eagerly testing them, we are spending time, energy and money in examining with astonishing and wearying particularity, the things we are doing now, counting our steps, doddering over the simple mechanics of our fine spun systems, and never saying to ourselves: "Let us do more and better things, though we smash, in so doing, all the petty rules we have established for ourselves in the past fifty years."[10]

In that simpler age, before library *service* became library (subsequently, information) *science*, there was a more realistic approach to standards; they were accepted and used, or rejected and ignored, solely on a pragmatic basis. The impact of standards was what librarians chose it to be. Was that good, or was that bad?

Standards in the Present

Times have changed, and in recent years standards have become far more important than they ever were. Too many librarians have accepted that they *must* be achieved. Standards have become ends in themselves and *the* solutions to all library problems. Only a few contemporary librarians, such as Hickey, retain any of Dana's skepticism about them. In suggesting that "it is possible . . . the uniformity which so often accompanies standardization can actually be a stultifying agent in the delivery of competent and imaginative local library service,"[11] Hickey stands almost alone. The flood of professional literature almost unanimously promotes the notion that standards are a good thing and decries that they have not been more readily and widely accepted and used.

I will not here recount all the current moves toward standardization or review the advocacy literature in detail. The best known and most intensive effort to promote library standards has been that of the American National Standards Institute's (ANSI's) Committee Z39 (Library and Information Sciences and Related Publishing Practices). ANSC Z39 takes the view that "with the advent of new and more complex technology in the information industry, further standardization will be essential if publishers, librarians, and information service professionals are to keep up in an increasingly more sophisticated market."[12] To that end it has promulgated some thirty-three standards for information agencies and has, according to its latest [as of November 1983] brochure, at least twenty-eight others under consideration. The latter include a Target Audience Code that will provide a standardized method for publishers to indicate the target audience of their publications. Obviously it will have to include an automatic designation of libraries of all types and sizes as a part of the target audience.

Nor is Z39 alone in its effort to promote standards. Almost every journal issue seems to report on a new activity, usually the formation of the inevitable committee. They range from SISAC (the Serials Industry Systems Advisory Committee), whose goal is "to develop and promote a standardized and automated system to facilitate the identification and processing of information concerning serials publications,"[13] to a series of new task forces (including one on performance measures) in the Association of College and Research Libraries (ACRL).[14] I am tempted to suggest the need for a standard for the development and implementation of standards, but that, I suppose, is what ANSI is all about.

Nothing is sacred. Cowan has recently noted:

> It is infinitely disturbing to discover, in more than one recent article advocating the need for standards in organizing and displaying infor-

mation, that formats other than the traditional 3 inches by 5 inches are recommended. These articles, in demanding new and stringent standards, are at the same time rejecting one of the truly great ones, treating it as though it had no inherent value.[15]

What Cowan fails to recognize is that the 3"-by-5" standard is itself relatively recent. I have in my collection of librarians two catalogs manufactured in the not-too-distant past by the Library Bureau—one is designed to hold 2"-by-5" cards and the other, 2"-by-3" cards.

As standards have become one of the primary panaceas for the ills of contemporary librarianship, the professional literature on the subject, naturally, has steadily increased. (Incidentally, whether it be standards, operations research, management review and analysis, or what-have-you, one should be inherently suspicious of any technique offered as a catchall solution.) Indicative of the importance placed on standards in library literature is the fact that in 1982 the editors of *Library Trends* saw fit to devote *two issues* to the topic. Those 358 pages of facts and figures tell more about librarians' fascination with standards than they do about the standards themselves. In that melange, only the excellent article by Paul and Givens—"Standards Viewed from the Applications Perspective"—which deals in some detail with the impact of procedural and technical standards, stands out. There the authors point out that

> librarians at every staff level abide by professional and process requirements which many of them accept with almost no recognition that they are specified in officially approved standards. Seldom are the requirements which are based on informally adopted standards distinguished from official standards directly regulating the activities of the library world or the world of other professions and service providers. This interrelationship of both intent and use makes it difficult to trace the direct use librarians make of many standards.[16]

Before I finally reveal my own view of the impact of standards on libraries, let me admit I have found, in addition to Hickey, one other contemporary librarian who takes a sane view of the subject. He suggests that

> we librarians, consciously or unwittingly, often impede progress by concentrating on trivia, ignoring the wider implications of change in technology and society, and being unduly parochial. Let us move forward . . . by taking the broader view, reinterpreting theory to match reality, and concentrating on the true ends and not the means. . . .[17]

I trust the reader will not be startled to learn that those comments were made by Michael Gorman, one of the chief architects of AACR2, the bold new cataloging standards.

The Impact of Standards

My own review of the professional literature confirms Paul and Givens' unfortunate finding that "a search of the literature reveals almost no discussion on the application of standards from the user's point of view."[18] Furthermore, there is no evidence in the literature that anyone has ever attempted to measure any aspect of the impact of standards. Whereas standards must be precise, librarians are asked to accept their value as an article of faith.

I do not argue that librarians need a standard for measuring the impact of standards. I do argue, however, that they need at least to give more thought to the effect of standards on their work and eventually to undertake some objective evaluation of them. Since so little has been done to date, I can only offer some subjective views on the impact of standards on library operations, using the following measures: *compatibility, cost, effectiveness and efficiency, production, quality*, and *service*. I challenge others to offer their own views, to adduce whatever evidence they might have. I ask them, however, to keep in mind Walter Nash's simple question, "Is that good, or is that bad?"

Compatibility

One of the primary goals in establishing library standards is to help ensure a certain level of uniformity. Uniformity will lead to compatibility—a worthy goal, but in a democratic society in which information policy and procedures are built slowly from the ground up, not always possible (nor desirable) to achieve.

In almost every aspect of their work librarians, and those who supply library materials, constantly seek new and better ways of doing things, using standards where they seem to work to advantage. But the search for a competitive edge can offset the effort to achieve standards. Videodisc is but one example of an information medium that has been crippled in the marketplace by incompatible systems. To expect widespread compatibility is an unrealistic expectation, and, in that respect, standards can have only a limited impact on libraries.

"Many of the existing generally accepted practices, so often mistakenly referred to as standards, are subject to interpretation by different individuals functioning in a variety of environments at different times and are controlled or motivated by differing conditions."[19] That interpretive latitude, as Wigington and Wood suggest, causes different libraries' cataloging records for the same publication to differ considerably. Efforts to upgrade the quality of standards—especially for manual systems—have led to "multiple superimpositions of standards and a resulting inconsistency of . . . structure and style. The idea of a standard is to impose consistency if not uniformity; yet the essentially organic nature of . . . [our tools] inhibits their complete renovation every few years."[20]

There is evidence that cataloging standards have enabled libraries for some time to use, if they chose to do so, other libraries' records to achieve some degree of uniformity and compatibility. Clearly the MARC formats, which have been widely adopted and used, are the most successful example of a standard designed to foster compatibility that has had, by any measure, a major positive impact on library work.

Cost

According to Wigington and Wood, the economic impact of standards has limited their utility. "In fact, even after useful ISO or ANSI Standards have been fully formalized, there is a long delay in getting them into widespread use, usually because of economic reasons."[21] Yet those same authors are among those who argue (but produce little evidence) that standards have improved the economy of library operations. Certainly, for example, the acceptance of standardized cataloging—first in the form of printed cards, or bibliographic information, from the Library of Congress, and more recently in the form of machine-readable records and national bibliographic services—has had a tremendous impact in reducing the rise of technical services costs, if not actually lowering the costs.

Unquestionably the development of more complex bibliographic standards to meet more complex needs and achieve greater compatibility has substantially increased the overall cost of information production. Since standards are a quest for perfection, they have undoubtedly contributed, on the whole, to the steady increase in the percentage of library budgets devoted to personnel, as opposed to that for library materials.

Effectiveness and Efficiency

Certainly librarians want standards, to help identify goals, set performance measures, and otherwise arrange and handle work in an effective and efficient manner. Although I can find no concrete evidence to prove the point, I admit that standards have had a major impact in this respect.

The question here is how effective and efficient librarians want to be, and the extent to which other qualities should be sacrificed to those goals. A good example is the oft-proposed but not yet accepted standard that would have publishers of serials place certain basic information in a standard format in a standard location on the covers of their publications. This standard would help libraries be more effective and efficient in handling the receipt and check-in of serials.

But serials are not cereal. The very process of distributing information depends on the publishers' ability to present the information in whatever manner is most effective for their (not librarians') purposes and to make changes, even from issue to issue, as they see fit. Noncompliance with a standard may have a negative impact on libraries, but librarians must respect the publishers' right to do so. One cannot sacrifice freedom of choice in favor of standards.

On the matter of efficiency, I will simply defer to an excerpt from "The Efficiency Expert" by my other library hero, Edmund Lester Pearson:

> "Look at your desk!" he went on.
> There I could obey him. . . .
> "It's the distance between your telephone and your hand I'm talking about. At least four inches too far to the left. Do you realize how much time and effort, how much efficiency, therefore, is lost by placing the telephone in the wrong position? Here is a report on the subject, which came in today. Bulletin No. 9, of the Sub-Committee on the Arrangement of Desk Fittings of the National Efficiency Congress in session all this week at Waukesha, Wis. They estimate that the loss of time, money and efficiency to the business men of the country by having the telephone too far to the left was over three million dollars in 1910 alone. It should stand eight inches from the left elbow—mark the place on your desk with a Maltese cross."
> "Suppose you move your elbow?"
> He did not hear me.
> "Now, the inside of the desk. The top drawer—yes, just as I expected. All wrong, all wrong. Should be divided into twelve compartments—this has ten. First compartment: Rubber bands—this has postage stamps in it. Next: pins—this has eyeglass case. All wrong. . . . I will set it right."
> He did so, and I have spent the rest of the week trying to find things.[22]

Production

Standards also enable us to measure production and devise means to increase output. They may be essential to improved production and, in that respect, can have a major impact on library work. At the same time it is ironic that so many large libraries are concerned about current levels of original cataloging output and are seeking ways to measure, control, and increase them.

Perhaps the detailed standards that have been adopted to put cataloging data into machine-readable form are so complicated they have become overly time consuming. Perhaps libraries need production standards because other standards have diminished librarians' ability to do their work.

Do production standards work in a library? Not entirely. They may work in areas such as book processing, where it is possible to control and measure the number of items handled, but to a large degree, especially in service areas, the flow of work is beyond control. To be effective one needs to be able to deal in the most expeditious fashion with whatever arises. Production standards, which may be rigidly interpreted as setting a maximum rather than a minimum, can result in stable levels of production but may not be responsive to peaks and valleys, or be conducive to the most efficient use of time.

Quality

How can librarians really measure what they do other than by the quality of the services they provide? The professional literature offers no evidence that anyone, even the most ardent standards advocate, suggests standards can improve quality. One of the few discussions of the relationship between quality and standards is in Lowell Martin's review of a new set of public library standards. Martin found, after a period of operation, that the greatest failure was in the lack of improvement in the quality of subject collections and service for the serious reader.[23]

Quality, always difficult to measure, consists, in a service field such as librarianship, of a variety of intangible features not subject to standardization. In fact, quality might be defined as a rising above standards.

Service

In at least one respect standards have enabled libraries to improve the level of service to users. The voluntary adoption, through participation in national bibliographic services, of standardized cataloging formats and records enables users to be reasonably sure that if they know how to find material in one library, they will be able to do so in another library. But reliance on that kind of standard may simply be easy for librarians; it may not best meet the service needs of clientele. To meet local needs, diversity in the arrangement and handling of material may sometimes be more appropriate and useful.

Carried to an extreme—as in recent efforts to promote international bibliographic control—it becomes more complex.

> Many international recommendations do reflect, on the one hand, librarians' will to bridge over the difference of national rules, but, on the other hand, they reflect their obvious hesitation to deny national traditions and characteristics.... Benevolently supposing that a worldwide exchange of authority files could be realized in the long run, at least by a number of great bibliographic agencies, the life-size question that remains is whether or not this would result in better service to the user. Is it is the interest of an English user to look for *Hikayat Bayan Budeman* instead of the *Tales of the Wise Parrot?*... In fact, the whole problem of international uniformity can be reduced to the question, Should the "bibliographic agency librarian" make descriptions primarily for his or her own public, adding UBC requirements as a kind of by-product, or should it be just the other way around?[24]

A Final Observation on the Present

I have not pretended to address all the ways in which standards affect library work, or to offer a balanced view. Rather, I have sought to raise some questions that should lead all librarians to ask whether the impact of standards is good or bad, to think more seriously about that question before they advocate and adopt standards.

The Future

What of the future of standards in library and information science? Most of the recent, voluminous literature suggests the need for greater attention to standards as a way of handling the ever-escalating volume of information and the many new forms it takes. There is something to be said for that point of view. There are also hazards awaiting us all in the wonderful machine future, and they will have an impact on how librarians approach and use standards.

In areas where librarians have had established standards that offer a certain element of security, changes will occur as professionals seek to improve the handling of information. Gorman points out, "All the major standards of our bibliographic life are under attack, subject to change and decay, and without obvious routes to success."[25] Just as librarians have mastered some complex standards, the standards may change. The impact of the changes will be increasingly costly and serious.

It is not just in arcane areas such as bibliographic control that standards are subject to change. The familiar layout of the QWERTY typewriter keyboard, which was devised in 1873 and became standard shortly thereafter, is now likely to be replaced by the Dvorak, or Alternative Keyboard for Alphanumeric Machines, which has been accepted by ANSI.[26] Fortunately that kind of change in a technical standard is, in the long run, easy to accommodate, as those who learned to operate the typing equipment under the old standard eventually die off.

Librarians are all familiar with the numerous problems created by new information formats that must be translated into reality through the use of technological devices. The profusion of information forms, and of the equipment to use those forms, will continue. There is no reason to believe standards soon will emerge to bring order out of this information chaos. Librarians will continue to be faced with difficult choices and are likely, individually and collectively, to spend substantial amounts of money on information systems that may disappear just as the relevant standards are emerging.

Recent events in Chad offer an interesting insight into the standards for the arrangement of names. In Chad the placement of given name and family name is a matter of personal preference. Those who live in French-influenced environments generally prefer the Western style of given name followed by family name; those who live in tribal environments often use the family name first and the given name second. It is a matter of personal choice, though, and no standard will help the cataloger faced with a book by a Chadian author.[27]

That may be the least of librarians' worries. Pool, a radical exponent of the future, suggests:

> The most important change [in the field of information] may be the end of the canonical text, produced in thousands of uniform copies. . . . Since Gutenberg, books, articles, manuals, or laws have been available in hundreds or thousands of locations in absolutely identical form. From that followed referencing; if you name the work, edition, and page, anyone anywhere can locate the identical thing. From that also followed catalogues and bibliographies.[28]

Electronic publishing, he suggests, will see a return to the fluid texts of the manuscript era.

Conventions will undoubtedly be developed for labeling variant versions, but there is no way of preventing their proliferation. If one can read a text (from wherever it originates) on one's own terminal, it means that that text has somehow been transmitted to one's own computer memory. Once there, it can be copied, modified, and retransmitted at will. The implications of all this for scholarship are mind-boggling. "Blue-sky" writing on the wonders of the computer age often describes how a scholar at his terminal will instantly be able to call up any book or article from the world's literature. Wrong. The proliferation of texts available in multiple forms, with no clear line between early drafts and final printed versions, will overwhelm any identification of "the world's literature."[29]

What will become of our carefully contrived standards? Where will we turn? Perhaps librarians will be able to take refuge in their first, and possibly their last, standard—the use of the alphabet as a means of organizing and arranging information under whatever name, in whatever shape or form, and in however many versions it may appear.

References

1. Sarah B. Ball, "Reminiscences of Things Past," *Special Libraries* 50 (1959):211-12.

2. J. W. Jolliffe, M. B. Line, and F. Robinson, "Why Libraries Differ—and Need They?" in *Organization and Handling of Bibliographic Records by Computer*, ed. Nigel S. M. Cox and Michael W. Grose (Hamden, CT: Archon Books, 1967), p. 62.

3. Jerrold Orne, "The Place of Standards in Libraries of the Future," *Bulletin of the Kentucky Library Association* 34 (January 1970):9.

4. Ronald L. Wigington and James L. Wood, "Standardization Requirements of a National Program for Information Transfer," *Library Trends* 18 (1970):433.

5. Don R. Swanson, "Evolution, Libraries, and National Information Policy," *Library Quarterly* 50 (1980):76-93.

6. Helen F. Schmierer, "Bibliographic Standards," *Annual Review of Information Science and Technology* 10 (1975):104.

7. Ibid., p. 106.

8. Lloyd W. Daly, *Contributions to a History of Alphabetization in Antiquity and the Middle Ages* (Bruxelles: Latomus, 1967), p. 25.

9. Arthur E. Bostwick, "Standardization," *Wilson Bulletin* 2 (1925):451-52.

10. John Cotton Dana, "Standardization in Libraries," *Wilson Bulletin* 2 (1925):453.

11. Doralyn J. Hickey, "The Search for Uniformity in Cataloging: Centralization and Standardization," *Library Trends* 25 (1977):579.

12. American National Standards Committee, *American National Standards*

Committee Z39: Library and Information Sciences and Related Publishing Practices, 1981, p. 1.

13. "Group Formed for Serials Standardization," *Wilson Library Bulletin* 57 (1983):554-55.

14. Carla J. Stoffle, "ACRL's New Task Forces," *College & Research Libraries News* 44 (1983):32.

15. B. Cowan, "Tongue in Cheek ... " *LITA Newsletter* 13 (Summer 1983):2.

16. Sandra K. Paul and Johnnie E. Givens, "Standards Viewed from the Applications Perspective," *Library Trends* 31 (1982):331.

17. Michael Gorman, "New Rules for New Systems," *American Libraries* 13 (1982):242.

18. Paul and Givens, "Standards Viewed" p. 325.

19. Wigington and Wood, "Standardization Requirements," pp. 434-35.

20. Hickey, "Search for Uniformity."

21. Wigington and Wood, "Standardization Requirements," p. 434.

22. Edmund Lester Pearson, "The Efficiency Expert," in Norman D. Stevens *Library Humor* (Metuchen, NJ: Scarecrow Press, 1971), pp. 183-84.

23. Lowell A. Martin, "Do the Standards Come Up to Standard?" *ALA Bulletin* 52 (1958):755-60.

24. Frans Heymans, "How Human-Usable is Interchangeable? Or, Shall We Produce Catalogues or Babelographic Towers?" *Library Resources & Technical Services* 26 (1982):160-61.

25. Gorman, "New Rules," p. 241.

26. Paul Katzeff, "Faster Than a Speeding QWERTY," *Boston Phoenix*, 26 April 1982, p. 7.

27. "What's in a Name? Whatever a Chadian Prefers," *Hartford Courant*, 17 August 1983, p. A11.

28. Ithiel de Sola Pool, "The Culture of Electronic Print," *Daedalus* 111 (Fall 1982):27.

29. Ibid., pp. 27-28.

RESPONSE

By Norman Vogt

Mr. Stevens has challenged us to think about how standards affect library work and whether they are good or bad. He is not really being irreverent (as he, with tongue in cheek, claims); he has simply assumed a questioning stance. And that is good. He is skeptical. And that is good.

How can librarians deal with their particular problems and not have some doubts about their work? In response to Mr. Stevens's challenge, I offer only my own views. I include some examples of how standards impinge on the work of a practicing serialist. This response might be called "A Selfish Look at the Impact of Standards on Libraries."

I define a standard as *a high and mighty rule (or set of rules) imposed by a chosen body of experts who establish rules (or a series of statements) to solve a particular problem for the good of all.* Before now I had not (to be perfectly honest) given much thought to how standards affected my professional life—the library business I engage in every day. But as I thought about the subject, and after I questioned my colleagues, it became clear that there is real concern for standards and how they affect day-to-day business in the library. This concern is not overwhelming, but it is nevertheless substantial.

It is clearer to me now than it was a week or so ago that librarians are affected by standards even when they are not aware of it. On a daily basis they deal with (though probably rather unconsciously), and are affected by, guidelines, policies, criteria, rules, and models. These policies and guidelines (or any other term one chooses to use) are really standards they themselves have established, or have been established for them to make their work easier.

Standards, like policies, can be adhered to or not. Librarians need to choose—based on their own needs, expertise, and experience—the appropriate course of action to pursue. They abide by a standard when it is to their advantage to do so, or when it serves them appropriately. For example, a librarian involved in union listing must be intimately acquainted with ANSI Standard Z39.42-1980, *Serials Holdings Statements at the Summary Level*, because it affords a basis for uniformity in a project which, without standardization, would founder in chaos. This is an example of a standard that grew out of a particular need and, I am told by those involved in union listing, is being widely used.

In *Serials of Illinois Libraries Online: Manual of Procedures* (affectionately known in Illinois as *SILO*), an entire 32-page chapter is devoted to an explanation of this ANSI standard and its application to SILO. Here, then, is the impact of a standard applied specifically to serials. I do not mean to imply it is a perfect standard. It is my understanding that this standard and the draft proposal of the *Standard for Serial Holdings Statements at the Detailed Level* are in some ways contradictory and that a combined standard to reconcile the differences is proposed. Perhaps the new standard will serve the needs of union listing even better than the old one.

Is it not the case that something evolves from weak to strong, is revised and updated until a workable product is achieved? If one uses the product (i.e., the standard) at its present stage, and uses it uniformly, and the result is consistency and ease of understanding, then the impact of that standard is good.

Other standards have affected my work as well. They are sometimes, but not always, directly related to serials. About two years ago, the ALA *Guidelines for Collection Development* (1979) were followed by our Collection Development Committee in creating a collection development policy. It would have been difficult, if not impossible, for a group of librarians, subject specialists, and academic department representatives to come to terms without those guidelines. They formed a "standard" around which a workable policy was developed.

Who would consider planning a new academic library building program without relying on the standards set forth in Keyes Metcalf's *Planning Academic and Research Library Buildings?* Our library faculty personnel committee relied heavily on the ALA *Model Statement of Criteria and Procedures for Appointment, Promotion in Academic Rank, and Tenure for College and University Librarians* as a model for our own standards.

Recently we received the ANSI *Standard for Ordering Single Titles of Library Materials*. This standard may be used in both monographic and serials acquisitions in our library. Another standard I have recently seen is the proposed ANSI *Standard for Claims of Missing Issues of Serials*. The use of these standards will, of course, be dictated by need.

One may think there are already too many standards, but I have heard the need expressed for a standard that would address "standardized" binding, the binding most commonly used in libraries today. The Library Binding Institute's *Standard for Library Binding* (1981) addresses what is typically called "Class A" binding only. The effect of a standard for the more commonly used binding would be better quality control and greater consistency. It would also provide guidance for comparisons of binding contract bids. And *not* having a standard adversely affects preservation, which is such a vital library concern today.

Serials standards may have very little impact on some libraries. For those that have manual serials systems, as perhaps most still do, standards may not be too meaningful. But looking to the future, as libraries move toward integrated, automated systems, standards will have a far more obvious impact.

One of the ideas Mr. Stevens expresses is not to carry standards too far but to use them to best advantage, as a means to an end. Perhaps serials librarians do carry things too far. Could it be that the serials mystique once again raises its head? Serialists might even go too far in expecting journal publishers to standardize the location of bibliographic information, even though it is the publisher's right not to. It would, however, be in librarians' best interest to encourage vendors to help them in this respect.

Standards serve the library community as well. They are tools designed to help. One does not, however, have to be a slave to them. They are a starting point. With them, librarians do not have to reinvent the wheel. Standards are good if one uses them for what one needs at the time—and that's not bad.

DEVELOPING TECHNOLOGIES AND THEIR IMPACT ON LIBRARIES: EIGHT TRENDS

By Thomas T. Surprenant

Librarians can examine developing technologies from at least two different perspectives. The first is to look at specific technologies and analyze their effects on the profession. This allows librarians to make day-to-day decisions based on a thorough knowledge of the capabilities of a particular technology. It is a very important part of library work because librarians are continually adopting technologies to improve their capacity to handle information.

The second perspective is to consider the systems or concepts the technology represents. This is a "macro" approach. It allows one to look at trends and long-term effects that are not dependent on a particular piece of technology but on the overall technological mix.

The move into the information age has resulted in a number of new technologies that promise to change the very basis of how librarians (and others) work. Yet the path is never clear, and there are many alternatives to examine. Not only is there a large number of alternatives to consider; one also has to deal with the ambiguities created by them.

When one takes a "macro" approach, a number of trends become apparent. I offer here a look at eight trends that have resulted from the introduction of new electronic media into the information environment.

I. The Tremendous Increase in Computer Storage Capacity and Decrease in Costs, with the Lag in Software Development

The twin phenomena of the continuing increase in computer storage capacity and the concomitant decrease in equipment costs are having a major impact on information handling and will have a significant effect on librarianship. One can expect the microcomputer (or, more correctly, the personal computer) to penetrate all levels of society and become as ubiquitous as the hand calculator.

National and international competition ensures that costs will continue to be low even as the technology improves. This is a highly volatile time; there are now over one hundred fifty major companies in the personal computer business, and a shakeout is inevitable. Osborne's bankruptcy signals only the beginning of an industry realignment.

In addition, the development of Very Large Scale Integration (VLSI) of circuits enables engineers to pack increased storage capacity into small computers. It will not be long before the entire contents of a 100,000-volume library can be stored in a VLSI chip or chips.

One of the axioms of the information age is that software lags behind hardware. Those who design new technologies in effect make declarations that have to be translated into software capable of realizing the promised capabilities, and software development takes time. This lag might be acceptable if the technology remained static, but that is not the case; new and improved versions are introduced with frightening regularity. Software that runs on one machine is not necessarily compatible with the new models. This incompatibility makes it hard to update and take advantage of technological advances. And this is only part of the issue. Software itself is being continually updated. With both the hardware and the support software in constant flux, it is extremely difficult to design and work with information systems.

II. The Development of Technologies to Decentralize Information, with an Increasing Need for Uniform Approaches to the Processing, Storage, and Transmission of Information

The electronic information grid is becoming increasingly complex as more and more computers are being added to the networks via telecommunications devices. Also, the increased numbers of computers, along with their growing sophistication, has resulted in information being collected to an extent never dreamed possible as little as twenty years ago.

The decentralization of information is threatening to disrupt the long-established communications channels that traditionally have directed its flow in society. Individual and custom-made data bases are beginning to appear. In some cases, the information is completely assembled by the data base originator; in other cases, it is down-loaded from existing data bases. Data bases frequently are customized to cater to a specialized user group. Decentralization imperils many societal institutions, including libraries, because the new channels of information bypass them.

To say there is a lack of uniformity in how information is processed, stored, and transmitted is a major understatement. Not only is this lack of uniformity discernible in the structure of information, it is also readily apparent in the technologies themselves, which don't always conform to agreed-upon standards. Progress has been made in some areas—AACR2, CP/M, and MS-DOS attest to that.

But now one begins to see, for each standard that has been established, a continuing round of exceptions that dilute and ultimately negate its effectiveness. As more and more information is added in a particular format, our ability, and willingness, to make changes and adjustments diminishes, even though the result is a decrease in our ability to handle what we have efficiently.

III. The "Electronic Cottage," Wherein More and More Work is Done, with the Gains of the Feminist Movement

In the move toward decentralization, the concept of the "electronic cottage" has come into being. Simply put, the "electronic cottage" revives the preindustrial age in which work was done at home. Information age activities and some societal norms lend themselves quite well to this concept. Work in the "electronic cottage" is very efficient in terms of savings in commuting costs and energy. It allows workers to live where they choose, thereby enhancing the quality of life. "Electronic cottage" workers can set their own work schedules to conform with their personal, day-to-day activities.

Working at home is said to be a positive influence on family life and can contribute to worker satisfaction, motivation, and productivity. One can expect a growing portion of the work force to exercise this option. It seems ideal for many library activities.

This concept is so full of paradoxes that any one of a dozen can be mentioned. Problems associated with the nature of work, creativity, supervision, and the worker himself or herself abound. In particular, the threat to the gains of feminism is an important concern. Recently, in conversation, a feminist librarian pointed out that the widespread adoption of the "electronic cottage" would drive women back into the home. She emphasized the historical abuses of cottage workers, citing examples of the sweat shops and piecework.

When one thinks about it, her fear seems justified. If librarians, as a profession, embrace this concept, those affected by it will predominantly be women. And many other parts of the information system employ women in large numbers as well. While it is too exaggerated to declare the "electronic cottage" a plot to force women back into the home, the actual effect could be the same. One has to take a hard look at this concept so it is not abused and at the same time make sure it remains a viable option for those who desire it.

IV. The Increase in "User-Friendly" Systems in the Electronic Environment, with the Recognition of the Need for More Human-to-Human Contact

One of the major breakthroughs in "user-friendly" systems came with the introduction of Apple's Lisa personal computer. But it was not the technology that was so significant; rather its importance derives from the recognition that users are not so interested in the *how* of the technology as they are in its direct *application* to their work.

This marks only the beginning of "user-friendly" systems. Many more will be introduced. They will decrease learning time and make it easy for the user to implement them in the work environment. The operative word here is "easy." Suddenly everyone seems to have recognized it as a critical element in the acceptance of new technologies, and the engineers are now paying greater attention to making their systems "friendly."

Some thinkers have speculated that we could end up as "electronic hermits." With both remote access to the world through an ever-expanding electronic grid and the increased "user-friendliness" of the technology, it has been posited that one could be born, work, and die within the confines of a single house or family compound without ever having to interact directly with other humans.

This fear, along with other general fears about the dehumanizing effects of technology, has alerted us to the need to be more attuned to ourselves as humans, to interact directly with each other. A book like the *Aquarian Conspiracy* makes us realize that a grass-roots, humanistic movement is growing in society.

As long as we have the proper perspective on how to implement the technology in such a way as to improve or ensure the quality of life, we have nothing to worry about. And as long as we keep a proper perspective on technology we can move toward a man/machine symbiosis that will preserve our humanistic values.

V. The Move into Electronic Publishing, with a Large Segment of the Information Industry Declining in its Ability to Purchase Information

Publishers have discovered the advantages of electronic technology as a means of selling information. Today, there are dozens of information services, periodicals, and at least one book available exclusively through the electronic grid. There seems little doubt that this is a growth industry directly tied in with the personal computer's pervasion of society. It is but a small step to increase dramatically the amount of information available to the public via direct electronic access. In fact, profits would likely go up if *direct* access were available, if it were not necessary for the public to use intermediaries like the library.

Electronic publishing comes at a bad time for the library profession. Declining budgets will be strained beyond the breaking point when money is needed to purchase the technological systems necessary to provide electronic access for users. This has already created problems with data base searching and the "fee versus free" debate.

Librarians may find themselves in a no-win situation. To hold onto the user group there will be a need to purchase the technologies to make access possible, which in turn will tend to decrease many library services currently provided. Thus, users may respond by going directly to the sources of information and not to the libraries. Not only might the user group erode but so might the amount of information available. The only solution to this dilemma is to increase budgets by proving that libraries are a necessary part of the information society.

VI. Computerized Data Bases Becoming Increasingly Complex, with the Bibliographic Utilities Dealing Directly with the User

The growth of information availability by means of the computer data base shows no sign of slowing. In fact, it is growing at such a rate that the bibliographic utilities are beginning to have a hard time providing timely access. As librarians have gained experience with the complexities of search-question construction and the peculiarities of specific thesauri, it has been necessary to limit their working knowledge to only a few selected data bases. There are just too many data bases for the librarian to know well enough to search them effectively.

To be able to develop and maintain the expert knowledge necessary for adequate searches, librarians have divided up the data bases. As the complexity of the information in the data bases increases and the sophistication of questions keeps pace, more and more time will be spent in search-question construction. Thus, helping the user will be a necessary part of the process.

Bibliographic utilities are shifting their emphasis and appealing directly to the user, bypassing the information intermediaries. This is not a new phenomenon; the utilities have always advertised in scientific and technical journals. But they have also realized that the growth of the personal computer market means increased personal access to the electronic grid. Since the bibliographic utility can be approached via a personal computer and a telephone link (modem), it is reasonable to provide the means for these users to do their own data-base searching. Personal searches have been encouraged by cheap rates and attempts to make the protocols more "user-friendly." Those who want to spend the time, and the money, to become proficient in one or more data bases now have opportunities to do so. Thus, libraries may ultimately find themselves in direct competition for users with the bibliographic utilities.

VII. Information as a Commodity, with the Need to Provide Information to Everyone

The age of information has put the spotlight on information itself. We have begun to realize the impact of the phrase "information is power." Part of the power of information lies in bundling it into salable packages and offering it to those who want it. While this is not dissimilar to traditional publishing, the new electronic technologies have created some real differences that enhance the view of information as a commodity.

More and more information is being collected, to an extent never before thought possible. In addition, there is ready access to the information via electronic technology. But most significant is the availability of software with which the user can manipulate the information once it is received. This customization, at all levels, creates a tremendous potential for entrepreneurs to repackage information for sale or use it in other profitable ways.

The terms "information-rich" and "information-poor" indicate the problem of information as a commodity. Those who can pay, or know how to gain access, are able to get what they need, and those who cannot don't. Again, this is not at variance with the present information structure. But the conversion of more and more basic (or survival) information into electronic form can, in effect, deny access to those who need it but cannot afford to pay.

This is a serious problem that will not be solved by libraries maintaining only those services that can be offered for free. This attitude limits library effectiveness and access to the growing mountain of information that will be available solely through electronic technology. Ways must be found to provide equitable access to information for all, and librarians should take the lead in attaining this goal.

VIII. The Development of Robots, Artificial Intelligence, and Knowledge Information Processing Systems, with a Surplus of Skilled Workers and a Decline in Support for Education

We seem to be jumping into the information age much faster than many expected. Hardly anyone predicted that home robots would be introduced much before the 1990s. Yet they were introduced in late 1982, and some say there will be more home robots than industrial robots in the very near future. Similarly, AI (Artificial Intelligence) and KIPS (Knowledge Information Processing Systems) are suddenly of great interest, an interest no doubt driven by the Japanese goal of controlling this aspect of technology by the end of the century.

These are areas where a great deal of promising research has been conducted, and most of the experts reside in the U.S. Both technological and economic developments have overtaken the field, and the competition will undoubtedly result in some startling advances in a few short years. If only a small portion of the goals are achieved, the societal changes that follow will be tremendous.

The move from an industrial to an information base has left, and will leave, a number of unskilled and highly skilled workers high and dry. We are doing a miserable job of remedying this problem. Retraining is a dire necessity, yet the commitment to this essential fact is next to nil. Not only is the educational system challenged at a time of budget declines, it is also charged with the responsibility for the failure of workers to have lifelong jobs.

It is safe to say there is no longer any such thing as a lifelong job. We will have to retrain a number of times throughout our lives. Thus, the educational system must restructure itself to the realities and train generalists who can become specialists for a time and then shift to another speciality.

This is especially true for librarianship. The remaining years of this century will be a time of high stress for the profession as it tries to cope with the electronic information environment. We may see a complete redefinition of the goals and activities of the library profession in relation to the advances in the electronic technology.

Conclusion

These trends illustrate some of the problems created by developing technologies as they relate to libraries. They are only a portion of the total
number we will be dealing with in the years to come. Those who survive
the coming years will have to be flexible in their approach to their work
as information professionals, as well as willing to take risks as new job
categories open up. It will be an exciting, challenging time that will have
to be weathered if librarianship is going to complete the transition into
the new age of information.

PUBLIC SERVICE STANDARDS FOR LIBRARIES

By James Rettig

Public services are nearly as much a part of everyday life as eating, sleeping, or breathing. They come from a multitude of providers, among them police departments, grocery stores, financial institutions, department stores, and transit authorities. The environment in which one operates affects a provider's need for service standards.

Most big city commuters have little choice but to continue to take the same bus or subway route twice daily, even if it means subjecting themselves to overcrowding, broken air-conditioning systems, and schedules honored more in the breach than in the practice. Transit authorities are relatively immune to the need to establish and enforce service standards. Grumble as they will about service deficiencies, most riders will continue to ride because they must.

Department stores, on the other hand—indeed, retailers in general—must, or at least for their own welfare should, establish and observe service standards. Customers who receive poor service at a store can and do express their displeasure by taking their business to competing stores.

Several examples will illustrate the difference. Recently I called my local gas company to establish service at my new address. After I explained my objective to the clerk who answered the phone, she asked me if I knew where my house would be. This absurd question was prelude to a laborious conversation in which my name, address, etc., all had to be spelled out several times before she recorded the information correctly. Were I able to heat my home by purchasing gas from another company, I would have terminated the exasperating conversation and called the competitor.

One time at a grocery store at 5.30 P.M. on a week night, I got into the "ten-items-or-less" checkout line. The basket of a customer several people ahead of me was bulging. The clerk and bagger gave that customer their routine greeting and then checked, tallied, and bagged his purchases.

When I came up with my fewer than ten purchases, I noticed that the bagger's name tag indicated he was also the store manager. So I asked why he permitted the customer to violate the ten-item limit. He said they found it was just easier to check such people through, and they did not want to alienate any of their customers. I assured him that his answer had alienated me and that in the future I would find it easier to patronize his competitors.

Libraries vs. Grocery Stores or Utilities

On the continuum of service providers, libraries stand much closer to grocery stores than to public utility companies. Surveys have shown that few people consider libraries to be their primary sources of information. They prefer to turn to friends or colleagues or rely on their own fallible memories for information. Furthermore, dissatisfied library users can withdraw their support.

These days the public is demanding greater accountability from publicly supported institutions. However unjustly, it places all the blame for the educational system's failure on teachers; the public's readiness to withhold salary increases from public school teachers is real, and teachers must recognize that. The public clearly wants performance from public institutions.

Libraries must perform, too, or the public will withhold funding from them. Public libraries are, of course, the most vulnerable. Special, school, and academic libraries, however, must also cultivate a constituency of well-pleased users who can influence the budget decisions of the libraries' parent organizations. The platitudes about the role of the library in society or in the educational enterprise are no longer unassailable; they must be validated by performance. In a recent article, Richard De Gennaro noted the transition libraries must make. He wrote:

> Contrary to the folklore of our profession, the real needs of library users are not for enormous and comprehensive collections of books and journals. The goal of amassing large collections comes from an earlier time when books and journals were fewer in number and less expensive. In the last two decades, the number of titles being published has exploded along

with their prices. The task for libraries, now and in the coming years, is to learn to be selective and to build lean, quality collections from the mass of printed and other materials that are gushing forth from the world's publishers. We also need to further develop our capabilities to gain effective access to materials that we do not and cannot have in our local collections as well as to resources in electronic form.[1]

But this is not enough. Services for users of these collections must become the library's focal point; otherwise, even "lean, quality collections" will become difficult to justify to any but ardent bibliophiles.

Microforms: Collections and Service

"*Microforms!*" Thus do the librarians at one public library I have used frequently link the user and the microfilm collection. When a user there wants an item on microfilm, the item must be paged. The librarian steps out from behind the reference desk, shouts "Microforms!" across a crowded reading room, and points to the patron who is holding the call slip for the desired item. The pointing is for the benefit of a page, a high school student who with a shuffling gait approaches the patron, wordlessly snatches the call slip, retrieves the film, mounts it on the reader, and then disappears. While standing there and being pointed at, one gets an idea of what it must feel like to be caught performing some obscene act. It takes courage to be a repeat user of microforms at that library.

Had I written "microforms" instead of "*Microforms!*" the reader undoubtedly would have thought of a collection of documents on film. Perhaps that was the reader's thought anyway. The words "serials" and "government documents" also conjure up images not of services but of collections. Standard introductory books on these forms of materials tend to ignore service questions.

Andrew Osborn's *Serial Publications* includes only a brief discussion of the problems incorrect or incomplete citations can create for reference librarians; he cites some examples.[2] Joe Morehead's *Introduction to United States Public Documents* fails to discuss reference work for government publications.[3] The chapter on reference in Yuri Nakata's *From Press to People* emphasizes reference books for access to government publications.[4] William Saffady's *Micrographics* skirts questions of service by speaking of little more than the microfilm reading room's physical requirements.[5] Sydney J. Teague's *Microform Librarianship* does no better.[6]

Microforms, serials, and documents librarians are very capable at servicing their collections. The books cited above imply, however, that these librarians are not much concerned about serving the public. The implication of De Gennaro's statement—that public service must receive far more attention from librarians—seems not to matter. Of course, this is an overstatement. Public service does matter to these librarians. One sign of its importance is the recent publication of Charles McClure and Peter Hernon's *Improving the Quality of Reference Services for Government Publications.*[7] The title, however, implies that service is not equal to the collections.

Libraries and librarians must perform and satisfy the public in order to survive in the current environment of skepticism about public service agencies. Therefore, it seems reasonable for librarians to want service standards they can invoke as proof of their worthiness. In creating service standards for themselves, it also seems reasonable for serials, documents, and microforms librarians to turn for guidance to the most publicly visible of public service librarians, reference librarians. What these librarians see when they look at reference librarians and their service standards will be reason for, if not dismay, then at least hesitation.

In the copious literature on library standards, one statement succinctly summarizes standards' twofold role:

> Standards for libraries generally are used for purposes of evaluation. Thus the task of designing a set of standards becomes the task of designing an instrument of evaluation. Standards are also designed to establish goals of excellence to be applied realistically by others.[8]

Evaluation of Reference Service

One frequently tried instrument of evaluation of reference service has been unobtrusive testing. In unobtrusive tests of reference service, the standard has been the accuracy of the information delivered by reference personnel (not necessarily professionals). Proxies pose questions, either in person or by telephone, and the test coordinator grades the librarians' responses.

The results of unobtrusive tests of reference have been universally dismal. In the best-known studies, the rate of accuracy hovers at about 50 percent. In their recent study of the accuracy of reference service for government publications in academic depository libraries, McClure and Hernon found an embarrassing 37 percent accuracy rate. The tests demonstrate that the accuracy rate varies considerably from library to library.

Clearly, reference librarians have not embraced accuracy as a standard or a measure for their service.

Insofar as the Reference and Adult Services Division of the American Library Association can be said to represent the consensus of American reference librarians, reference librarians have embraced "A Commitment to Information Services: Developmental Guidelines."[9] Approved in 1976 and expanded in 1979 to include a statement on ethics, this document describes general guidelines; it does not lay down standards. More than just reference librarians should at least consider these guidelines, how-ever, for they "are directed to all those who have any responsibility for providing reference and information services."[10] They serve more to establish goals of excellence than to create an instrument of evaluation.

The few statements in the guidelines that are measurable are either/ or situations, such as the requirement for "a published service code."[11] Either a library has "a published service code" or it doesn't. For the most part the document is hortatory, leaving vague the goals for excel-lence that true standards would define. Even the section on evaluation is vague.

Evaluation of services is at best very difficult. Reference service has proved to be especially intractable.[12] One major difficulty has been in judging what constitutes reference service and, therefore, what is to be measured and evaluated. Simply defining reference service as 'answer-ing questions' is far too narrow and restrictive. Answering questions is only the reactive aspect of reference work. Success in it depends not only on the qualifications of the personnel but also to a great extent on the reference staff's active efforts, especially in building a responsive reference collection.

A means of evaluating reference collections needs to be devised so that standards for their scope, currency, and relation to other collections in a library can be written. Thus, simply measuring output (i.e., the proportion of questions answered correctly) ignores other significant factors. One is the collection. Another is the *process* of answering questions.

Process: Time and Manner

This process is multifaceted. One significant facet is time. In their study of documents reference service, McClure and Hernon found that li-brarians in the Northeast who spent more time on questions provided right answers a higher percentage of the time. To confound matters, they also learned that in the Southwest the longer librarians spent on a question, the more likely they were to answer it incorrectly.[13]

Perhaps patrons have a tolerance for error as long as service is speedy. But surely speed is relatively less important than accuracy when the accuracy rate for questions dealt with quickly is only about 50 percent. Speed of service is more significant for serials and microforms than for reference and documents librarians. This is because most transactions at serials and microforms desks are for known items rather than requests—so common in general and documents reference work—for "information about x."

Another significant factor is the service provider's manner. This can be very important to patrons or customers of a public service. Even when one receives the service desired, if it is rendered in a rude or disagreeable manner, the recipient will sometimes perceive the encounter as a failure. Think of the times when the surly manner of a waiter or waitress has spoiled your enjoyment of a well-prepared meal.

In an unobtrusive test of telephone service at the University of Minnesota, in which the library's general reference division gave correct answers 60 percent of the time, the proxy patrons reported the librarians were pleasant 95 percent of the time. Ninety percent of the proxies were satisfied enough with the service that they would use it again.[14] Evidently manner more than accuracy influenced the proxies' judgment on this point.

In the same study, the library's maps division earned only a 50 percent accuracy rate, though its librarians were pleasant 80 percent of the time. Only 70 percent of the proxies would call the maps division again for information. One can infer that both accuracy *and* manner are important to patrons.

Another effort to judge reference librarians' manner, this one at the general reference desk of the University of Oregon library, was inconclusive.[15] Researchers could not separate patrons' good mood after the reference encounter from their satisfaction with the answers to their questions.

Nonetheless, "how" is every bit as important as "what" in providing public services. Outcries about police brutality committed by officers performing otherwise legitimate police duties are an extreme example of the importance of the manner in which service is rendered. One's personal boycott of a store (or perhaps a library) where service is consistently brusque or rude is a less dramatic expression of the importance of manner.

Complexity and Accuracy Tests

One unobtrusive test sought to measure librarians' willingness to negotiate complex questions.[16] In 67 percent of the encounters, the librarians took at face value a question such as: "Where can I find your books on poetry?" In only 20 percent of the encounters did they interview the patrons enough to pass through an intermediate step and ultimately arrive at the real need expressed by that question. The proxy in this case really wanted a definition of concrete poetry.

On the whole, then, reference librarians' practice does not provide standards for public service. And yet they have no choice but to work with the materials at hand.

One item not reported explicitly in the unobtrusive studies is the range of overall accuracy of individual libraries. It is, however, known to vary considerably. Through a close reading one can learn that in McClure and Hernon's study at least one library answered at least 70 percent of the questions correctly.[17]

Additional unobtrusive testing should be done to identify the most successful libraries. These libraries can then be studied in depth to determine why and how they excel. McClure and Hernon identify variables requiring further study. Their list, which follows, has been modified here to eliminate specific references to documents work:
- The number of reference questions received by staff members in the average workday or week
- Staff salaries
- Familiarity with the reference collection
- The academic degrees of the participants
- The number of hours the department is open for public service
- The training of paraprofessionals
- The average number of hours spent answering reference questions each week
- Professional activities (number of conferences and workshops attended, reading professional literature, etc.)
- Expenditures for reference materials
- Adequacy rating of reference collection in terms of comprehensiveness, currency, scope, depth, and other criteria[18]

All these variables can be applied to specialties within librarianship that have public service responsibilities. Unobtrusive testing of the accuracy of serials and microforms desks in fulfilling user requests could be as enlightening as it has been for general or documents reference work.

Evaluating Service

The need to give greater emphasis to the service aspects of serials and documents work has not gone unnoticed, even if it has been understated. Several years ago, Helen Grochmal pointed out:

> Even when·a person has been helped by a reference librarian with bibliographic reference sources and comes to the serials department prepared with a specific serial citation, the person may still need more than directional assistance.[19]

And Steven Zink, now a member of the Depository Library Council, has stated, "Over the years government publications departments, due to staff shortages or traditional non-interest, have been shockingly inactive in explaining, promoting, and attempting to make understandable their available services."[20]

Unobtrusive testing plus follow-up testing of the most accurate libraries hold promise for all public services in libraries. On the findings of such research the profession can establish standards for services. Differences in the "how" of successful libraries and the service of less accurate libraries may point out what constitutes good services. These factors can then be codified in standards.

Value of National Standards

It remains foolish, however, to expect national standards for public services. Further attempts at such statements probably cannot be any less vague or platitudinous than either the RASD's "A Commitment to Information Services" or the Depository Library Council's "Guidelines for the Depository Library System." Thus a different approach, one that utilizes the research data gathered through unobtrusive testing and other studies, offers libraries their best hope as a foundation for standards.

The ARL-ACRL "Standards for University Libraries," endorsed by ARL in 1978 and approved by ACRL in 1979, suggests a way such research data could be put to practical use in establishing public service standards.[21] The appendix to the university library standards describes quantitative analytical techniques that can be used to compare institutions.

These same techniques could be used to compare specific measures of a library's service performance to that of similar libraries identified as being among the best service providers. A library would then know how its services rate and could make needed changes. One hopes that over time the best institutions would analyze their own performance and improve, thus encouraging improvement on down the scale.

Identifying precisely those factors in need of improvement would be difficult, of course. This places great faith in research. It is probably not a misplaced faith, and indeed, after more than a century of reference services in libraries, it is clear that other means will not yield adequate service standards for either individual libraries or the profession as a whole.

Meanwhile, librarians must think more about the "how" of their public services. They must depend on library users to help them judge the tenor and quality of their services, just as profit-making companies use market research to judge their services. One promising but little-used technique of getting user input on the relative importance of time, accuracy, staff attitudes, etc., is conjoint analysis.

A promising application of conjoint analysis was described in a paper by Michael Halperin and Maureen Strazdon.[22] In addition to ranking the relative values of service factors, conjoint analysis can also indicate "the value of various alternatives related to any single aspect"[23] of service, for example, patrons' sensitivity to a price increase for computer searches or interlibrary loans. The technique is somewhat cumbersome as it involves a sample of users who must complete questionnaires ranking aspects of service. It can be tailored, however, to a particular library's situation.

Experimenting with Standards

Research takes time, but the public's demand for accountability will not wait. So in the meantime, librarians must experiment with various service practices. I have yet to hear of a reference desk that assures the equitable treatment of patrons by having them queue and wait for the next available reference librarian as is done in banks and at airport check-in lines. I do know, however, of a busy reserve desk that uses a number system as in bakeries.

Librarians would do well to examine the practices of other service providers. Contrast one fast-food chain's policy of not serving any food prepared more than seven minutes earlier, to a public library's policy forbidding librarians to spend more than five minutes on any reference question. The first policy guarantees uniform quality; the second policy guarantees a good number of failures.

One discount department store in Chicago routinely opens another checkout line if more than three customers are in any other line. How many libraries have attempted such flexible public service staffing? Libraries must be less *re*active and more active in delivering information and research services. The public will judge libraries by what they provide and how they provide it. The effort to establish service standards is worthwhile and necessary. Standards must be realized by every librarian.

Individuals and Quality Service

McClure and Hernon concluded that "the individual library staff member *is the single most significant factor* affecting the quality of reference service for government documents."[24] Nevertheless, it is true that in unobtrusive testing some libraries consistently perform better than others. One hopes that when these libraries are singled out, their staff members will develop an even deeper concern for the quality of their service. Not content to rest on their laurels, they will, one sincerely hopes, strive for improvement.

Childers found that librarians in an individual library are often governed not by library service policies but by personal policies. Perhaps in libraries serious about the quality of their service, peer example or, if need be, supervisory or peer pressure will eliminate conflicting personal policies that lead to inferior service.

It is embarrassing but true that some persistent patrons have discovered that their questions, answers to which were attempted unsuccessfully by one librarian, can sometimes be answered if they return to the library when a different librarian is on the reference desk.

Service standards in a library should be consistent. Public service standards developed through testing and analysis of the results could "establish goals of excellence to be applied realistically by others" both inside and outside the library.

A few brief examples underscore the need to make the effort to evaluate reference and other public services and establish standards for service. One of McClure and Hernon's proxies reported that

> the librarian had an interesting attitude towards the indexes in her collection. She portrayed them as difficult and unfathomable. There was one that she knew of as the 'PRthingy" [PRF] but would not use because she was unfamiliar with it.[25]

Childers reported the following exchange:

"Can you tell me who makes X?"
"I'm sorry, this is a library. I don't know."[26]

Not as dramatic but more telling, because it was a question asked in real need rather than as a part of a test, was what occurred when I recently answered the phone at my library's reference desk. The caller identified herself as calling from another state. She needed biographical information about Sandra J. Hirstein. A librarian at the caller's local library had used the *National Faculty Directory* to identify Hirstein as a faculty member at my university. A check of several university directories showed that a James J. Hirstein is on the faculty at another campus of the university. A quick check of the *National Faculty Directory* showed that it gave this same information. The librarian elsewhere had completely botched the question and cost the patron a long-distance call.

These are harsh examples, yet similarly poor service may well be typical, test results tell us, as much as half the time. The single study of a special group of service providers, documents librarians, showed a worse rate. One wonders what the rate is at microforms and serials desks and fervently hopes it is better.

This paper opened with a commercial analogy; thus it is appropriate to close with one. In his famous article "Personal Relations Between Librarians and Readers," the first exposition of reference service, Samuel Green wrote: "A librarian should be as unwilling to allow an inquirer to leave the library with his question unanswered as a shop-keeper is to have a customer go out of his store without making a purchase."[27] Good advice in 1876, and every bit as good today!

References

1. Richard De Gennaro, "Theory vs. Practice in Library Management," *Library Journal* 108 (July 1983):1321.

2. Andrew Osborn, *Serial Publications: Their Place and Treatment in Libraries*, 3d ed. (Chicago: American Library Association, 1980).

3. Joe Morehead, *Introduction to United States Public Documents* (Littleton, CO: Libraries Unlimited, 1975).

4. Yuri Nakata, *From Press to People: Collecting and Using U.S. Government Publications* (Chicago: American Library Association, 1979).

5. William Saffady, *Micrographics* (Littleton, CO: Libraries Unlimited, 1978).

6. Sydney J. Teague, *Microform Librarianship*, 2d ed. (London: Butterworths, 1979).

7. Charles R. McClure and Peter Hernon, *Improving the Quality of Reference Service for Government Publications* (Chicago: American Library Association, 1983).

8. Beverly P. Lynch, "University Library Standards," *Library Trends* 31 (1982):46.

9. "A Commitment to Information Services: Development Guidelines," *RQ* 18 (1979):275-78.

10. Ibid., p. 275.

11. Ibid., p. 276.

12. For good recent summaries of unobtrusive tests of reference and other evaluation techniques, *see*: F. W. Lancaster, "Evaluation of Reference Service," in *The Measurement and Evaluation of Library Services* (Washington: Information Resources Press, 1977). *See also* Ellen Altman, "Assessment of Reference Services," in *The Service Imperative for Libraries: Essays in Honor of Margaret E. Monroe*, ed. Gail A. Schlachter (Littleton, CO: Libraries Unlimited, 1982).

13. McClure and Hernon, *Improving the Quality*, p. 47.

14. Geraldine B. King and Rachel Berry, *Evaluation of the University of Minnesota Libraries Reference Department Telephone Information Service. Pilot Study* (Arlington, VA: ERIC Document Reproduction Service, 1973). [ED 077 517]

15. Wyma Jane Hood and Monte James Gittings, *Evaluation of Service at the General Reference Desk, University of Oregon Library* (Arlington, VA: ERIC Document Reproduction Service, 1975). [ED 110 038]

16. Thomas Childers, "The Test of Reference," *Library Journal* 105 (April 15, 1980): 924-28.

17. McClure and Hernon, *Improving the Quality*, p. 68.

18. Ibid., pp. 82-83.

19. Helen M. Grochmal, "The Serials Department's Responsibility for Reference," *RQ* 20 (1981): 403.

20. Steven D. Zink, "The Impending Crisis in Government Publications Reference Service," *Microform Review* 11 (1982):109.

21. "Standards for University Libraries," *College & Research Libraries News* 40 (April 1979):101-10.

22. Michael Halperin and Maureen Strazdon, "Measuring Students' Preferences for Reference Service: A Conjoint Analysis," *Library Quarterly* 50 (1980):208-24.

23. Ibid., p. 210.

24. McClure and Hernon, p. 111. [Emphasis in original.]

25. Ibid., p. 134.

26. Childers, p. 927.

27. Samuel S. Green, "Personal Relations Between Librarians and Readers," *Library Journal* 1 (1876):79.

RESPONSE

By Leigh Chatterton

In preparing these remarks, I found I really had two very distinct reactions to what Mr. Rettig has written—the first to the need for public service standards, and the second to the view that serials, documents, and microforms librarians are more concerned with their collections than with public service.

With regard to the need for public service standards and standards in general, there really is nothing new I can add to what has already been so ably presented. I would like to emphasize, however, a few of the thoughts that went through my mind as I read Mr. Rettig's paper.

Yes, we need standards! Especially in view of the increasing number and variety of cooperative efforts of which libraries are a part. Yes, the development of standards is a difficult and time-consuming task, but it *must* be accomplished if libraries are to have any hope at all of surviving in the years to come.

At the same time, let us not forget that each and every library is an entity unto itself. It has its own needs, its own problems, its own collections, and, most importantly, its own patrons—and *all* these factors must be taken into account not only when a standard is to be implemented in the library but also when it is under development.

Finally, if necessary, libraries must have the courage to modify or even ignore the standards. This is especially true in cases where standards will in effect prevent the libraries from providing those services they are meant to provide.

In summation, standards are good and they are bad, but most importantly, they are facts in a library's life with which librarians must learn to deal successfully.

My second reaction is to the view that serials, documents, and microforms librarians are more concerned with their collections than with public services. Where serials are concerned, this view may well have been true a few years ago—especially in light of the fact that serials operations have traditionally been considered a part of technical services' support operations and not a public service operation—but it is not the case today.

With the development of automated serials control systems such as Ebsconet, Linx, and OCLC's serials control subsystem, as well as the interlibrary loan and union list functions associated with Linx and OCLC, to mention just a few, more and more serials librarians have ready access to an abundance of information and are able to satisfy their users' needs not only within the serials department but elsewhere as well. Indeed, many libraries, such as those at Appalachian State, Boston University, and Houston Public Library, already provide rather extensive public service for their serials collections.

But what of the documents and microforms librarians? Though I have not had extensive contact with them, the little I have had has shown me they are working very hard to provide the best possible public service. Unfortunately, they do not have sufficient staff or other alternatives available to allow the quality of public service their collections demand.

Despite these obstacles, attempts are being made to increase hours of service, establish information service desks, and bring collections together with the proper equipment and reference tools needed for their full use. Obviously, these are all changes aimed at improving public service in the documents and microforms areas.

In conclusion, I think it fair to say that while the past may show serials, microforms, and documents librarians to have been more interested in their collections than in public services, this is most assuredly not true today. Librarians know they have to improve their services. They have made great gains in the last few years, and fully intend to continue to do so in the future.

DEVELOPING PERFORMANCE STANDARDS FOR LIBRARY STAFF

By Ronald G. Leach

Over the years I have been involved in personnel systems at several universities. Each of these systems has had as major components salary schedules, position classifications, job descriptions, and annual evaluations (including those for promotion and tenure). But as I think back, none of the systems had performance standards as a formal component of the personnel system. There probably were some performance standards in operation, but they were likely to have been verbal and not an ongoing part of the annual evaluation.

Since I have not developed formal performance standards or worked extensively with them, I have approached this topic as I would any major issue I face in my position as Dean. This approach is to pose several questions and then seek the answers from selected literature, discussions with colleagues, and other sources. Let me hasten to add that my examination of the professional literature and my discussions on the subject were not exhaustive.

Why Performance Standards?

The first question I asked was: "Why should one be concerned with performance standards?" There appear to be at least four reasons: *First*, when one examines academic library expenditures one finds that personnel have been, and continue to be, the most costly component of a library program. In fact, in many large university libraries, they may represent 65 to 70 percent of the total budget.

Every aspect of a library's activities is determined by the competence, motivation, and general effectiveness of its human organization. Yet, interestingly enough, not much attention is given to the appraisal of this resource. Or, if attention is given, not much about it is appearing in library literature. Far more concern is directed to the acquisition, organization, and storage of collections. Perhaps the large expenditure for personnel is reason enough to be concerned about the value of performance standards, but there are others.

The *second* reason for considering the subject is that academic libraries, like their parent institutions, are under increasing pressure to be more accountable and productive. This pressure is being exerted by legislatures and government leaders at a time when most colleges and universities are facing retrenchment due to enrollment declines.

Librarians are being asked to do the same, or more, with less than they are accustomed to, and, in the minds of many, it can no longer be business as usual. In a sense they are being forced to review the how, why, how much, how soon way of doing things, and to that end, performance standards may be worth considering.

The *third* reason for considering performance standards is the prevalence of automation in libraries today and its projected growth in the future. Librarians are using technology more and more as a tool of their trade. It has appeared in almost every aspect of library operations. Oddly enough, this new tool now enables librarians to keep track of their activities and may for the first time allow them to cull information that could be useful in the development of performance standards. In other words, now that librarians are using automation, they may be able to generate information more easily to implement performance standards as part of the personnel system.

According to the literature, the *fourth* reason is that performance standards make an annual appraisal more effective. My reading indicates that a good performance appraisal system provides employees with (1) information on what is expected of them, (2) information on what performance standards are being used, and (3) regular feedback regarding progress, or lack of progress, toward individual and unit goals and objectives.

Performance standards *do* help employees to know what is expected of them. They also enable the supervisor to overcome the so-called halo effect (what has this employee done for me lately?) and focus on year-round performance. In addition, they require the supervisor to review all performance components rather than concentrate on the few he or she feels are most important.

It seems to me the four reasons outlined above are sufficient for academic libraries at least to consider whether or not performance standards should be a formal part of their personnel systems.

What Is a Performance Standard?

The next questions I asked were: "What is a performance standard, and how does it differ from goals, objectives, performance appraisal, job description, and other related components of a personnel system?" It is important to try to define performance standards before trying to determine how they differ from something else. They are "written statements of conditions that will exist when a job is being well done." They make employee "role expectations" explicit in terms of qualitative and quantitative levels of performance to be achieved; they become yardsticks against which actual performance can be measured.

In other words, performance standards have components of *measurability, time,* and *attainability* that are written down so they can serve as criteria by which performance can be judged. Individual performance standards set the acceptable level of individual performance and are usually quantifiable, e.g., the interval between the acquisition of material and its being forwarded to the cataloging unit. (Please note that the theme of "measurability" runs throughout these descriptions.)

Goals and objectives also have a degree of measurability, but they differ from performance standards in that the latter are usually more specific, describe desired results, and are ordinarily developed to measure individual performance.

Job descriptions, although closely related, also differ from performance standards. Whereas they set forth what is to be done on the job— that is, what functions or tasks are to be performed—performance standards describe "how much" or "how well" or the "acceptable level" at which the job is to be performed.

Performance standards are also closely related to performance appraisals. Whereas the former establish criteria for the acceptable level at which a job is to be performed, performance appraisal is the actual process of evaluating whether an individual actually meets the established standards. In other words, the job description describes the requirements of a particular job; the performance standards establish the acceptable levels of job performance; and the performance appraisal is the formal process of determining—both qualitatively and quantitatively—whether an individual has done the job satisfactorily.

Contents of Performance Standards

There are several components and characteristics that should be observed if one decides to develop performance standards. The first major component of an effective standard is a "measure." It can be stated in various terms such as dollars, percentages, numbers, ranges, and so forth. When incorporating it into performance standards one should avoid using descriptive terms like "approximate," "few," or "reasonable." Instead, *specific measures* should be used.

The second major component is "time." Time should be involved in every standard, even though it is itself a measure. Time provides a framework within which the attainment of the standard will take place.

"Attainability" is the third component that should be incorporated into a performance standard. A performance standard should, without question, be within the individual's reach. If fiscal constraints or organizational policy will preclude the attainment of the standard, then the standard should not be written.

Let me give an example using all three components. If one develops a standard that reads: "Manages department expenses within plus-or-minus 2 percent of annual budgets"—

the *measure* component is . . . plus-or-minus 2 percent

the *time* component is . . . annual

the *attainability* component is . . . whether or not it is possible to manage expenditures within the given range.

While these three major components may be incorporated into a standard to aid in evaluating performance, there is another factor more difficult to incorporate—a measure of *quality*. It is clear that some activities or tasks in the library are more easily quantifiable than others. It is one thing to write a standard to measure numbers and time; it is quite another to write one to measure quality.

If, for example, a cataloger can catalog the established number of units in the established time period, there still has to be some way to assess the quality of the work performed. The literature (other than in references to "errors") is not helpful about how to measure quality. And, how does one measure the "quality" of an answered reference question? This is the perennial question asked by reference librarians.

Developing and Implementing Standards

First one should consider who ought to develop the standards. One option is for the supervisor to write them. This probably is the most efficient method in terms of time spent on the task. In some instances, it may have to be chosen. The major problem with this approach is that standards written by the supervisor are "owned" by the supervisor, not the employee.

A second approach is to hire a consultant to develop the performance standards. Again the question of ownership is likely to arise, neither the supervisor nor the employee feeling the standard is his or her own.

The third approach is for the supervisor and employee to identify and agree on the key areas that should receive attention during a given period. Then the supervisor, or preferably the employee, should write a draft of the standards. Again, agreement is sought, and the supervisor reviews the individual performance standards to be sure they support the goals and objectives of the unit and organization.

My own experience in managing personnel during the past thirteen years would lead me to select the third (or participative) approach, if possible. By it the supervisor obtains a better commitment from the employee because the employee has some "ownership" through his contribution to writing the standard.

There are a number of factors I found in my reading that may be useful for a library to consider if it decides that performance standards should be developed:

1. Recognize that developing performance standards takes time. Performance standards for lower-level clerical positions may be completed in hours; more complex or higher-level positions may take days.
2. Start with a position description to review the position's overall duties, accountabilities, and responsibilities.
3. Examine past performances, successes of colleagues, and other performance benchmarks.
4. Keep in mind the goals and objectives of the unit and organization.
5. Meet with the employee to identify and seek agreement on areas that should receive attention during the performance period.
6. Encourage the employee to write the first draft of what he or she thinks are satisfactory performance standards.
7. Finalize agreement on the performance standards.
8. Build in a periodical review cycle to ensure that the standards are realistic, achievable, and contribute to the library's service objectives.

Pitfalls in the Implementation of Performance Standards

It would be nice if there were no negative aspects to report on the development of performance standards, but there are. There are a number of pitfalls to avoid. They include:

1. Failure to realize that the development and implementation of standards takes a lot of time. If, however, standards would improve productivity and communication, then perhaps the time would be a good investment. These factors should be considered before any decision is made to develop standards, as management experts say it takes up to *three years* of experimentation and adjustment to establish good performance standards.
2. Failure to recognize the added costs of administering performance standards. There will be additional costs involved in administering the standards and training supervisors and employees in their development and use. Of course, there are similar costs in beginning any new process; in that respect, developing performance standards is no different.
3. The temptation to take shortcuts, such as adopting some other library's standard. If a manager hurriedly develops some superficial standard or copies someone else's, it will likely result in little or no commitment on the part of the employee or the manager.
4. Another difficulty encountered is how to determine at what level a standard should be set. If standards are set too high, they may be unattainable, and the employee may become discouraged and resentful. If they are set too low, it may be difficult to "negotiate" them upward. Considerable effort should be made to define and establish performance standards at a "satisfactory" level and establish parameters for various levels of above-satisfactory performance.
5. There is the pitfall of setting standards for the individual, not the position. Supervisors have to be mindful that performance standards are set for the position, not the person. Failure to keep the standards consistent for employees in the same level position can result in the employee feeling that the evaluation is unfair.
6. There is the pitfall of thinking that standards must be written for every aspect of a position, yet in libraries there are certain aspects of supervisory or clerical performance that defy quantification. For example, how can one write a quantitative standard to measure a receptionist's skill in greeting visitors or measure a reference librarian's manner in helping patrons at the desk? One can't. Instead, the manager (and employee) have to make an evaluation by applying subjective judgment.
7. The last pitfall is what I call the failure to deal with human concerns. Implementing performance standards is instituting change, and people naturally resist change.

Human Concerns and Standards

Some employees may react negatively when the concept of performance standards is first introduced. In fact, if performance standards are imposed on members of an organization in dictatorial fashion, the organization can expect strong resistance. On the other hand, if performance standards are established through formal negotiation between the individual employee and his or her supervisor, then the employee has a stake in the standards and may be more willing to make a commitment to their implementation and use.

There is no substitute for face-to-face dialogue and staff participation in developing performance standards. My recommendation to any manager thinking about developing performance standards is to adopt a basic change strategy to "create conditions where those affected by the change can play a meaningful role in planning and carrying it out." In other words, have the staff participate in developing the standards.

If the manager does not seek a staff member's participation, he may meet resistance. This response might be typified by a statement I overheard at a library where the administration had decided to institute performance standards. A librarian said, when they [the administration] first told me "they were going to develop standards to measure my performance, I felt angry. I had worked in my position for more than ten years and from all indications had been doing a good job. Now they suddenly want to measure me." She went on to say that "after two or three weeks I began to think about why it might be necessary or good for the library to develop performance standards and I became less angry." Still later, after more explanation, she said, "I began to see the potential value of such standards."

My reason for mentioning this particular case is that employee anger, or at least suspicion, is probably typical. Fortunately, this staff member moved from an emotional to an intellectual or rational response to the development of performance standards. My feeling, without knowing all the details of the situation, is that the library administration had not done a very good job of communicating with, or involving, the staff in the change, at least in the early stages. The risk any administrator takes in not involving staff is that their resistance to change may remain at the emotional level.

Performance Standards in Libraries

The concept of assigning employees a specific amount of work to be completed within a specified time is not new in the business world.

Performance standards are, however, contrary to the previous orientation of many library managers and staff. In the past library managers have not been as concerned with measuring specific results as they are now. For example, I have read many appraisals that did not have performance standards as a basis, and they sounded somewhat like this:

> Jim has continued to perform in an exemplary manner. His performance has been continually marked with strong initiative. He has repeatedly been willing to tackle problems in the catalog department and is well liked by other staff.

If the library had been using performance standards developed jointly by Jim and his supervisor, they both could monitor Jim's progress, which might have been reported like this:

> Jim has made a significant contribution to the cataloging department. He has completed an average of 8 original cataloging titles per day. The standard is 6. In addition, his error rate has dropped 5%, and the quality of thought he brings to departmental problems results in his recommending good, sound, and logical solutions.

The point of this illustration is in the latter description. There the individual's performance evaluation depends more on results based on predetermined standards that were, one hopes, developed jointly by supervisor *and* employee, rather than based on personality, seniority, or some other subjective factor.

Properly understood and planned performance standards can be helpful in establishing a common understanding between supervisor and staff member about what is expected from the position. They also can help improve the library's overall performance, *if* the process is open and staff members are involved.

Each library administration and staff will have to decide if performance standards should be a component of their personnel system. Perhaps this discussion about what performance standards are, what components should be included in them, what steps are involved in developing and implementing them, and what pitfalls to avoid will offer some initial guidelines.

RESPONSES

By William J. Willmering

As a supervisory librarian in a serials department of nine professional and thirteen support staff, I have been involved in the development of performance standards for all grades over the last three years. And I concur with what Dr. Leach has outlined in his paper. The time factors, the supervisory overhead, and, above all else, the human concerns—all are important factors in the development of performance standards. But I have found several other factors, not mentioned by Dr. Leach, that I believe are important.

In the National Library of Medicine, the reason for initiating performance standards was simple. Congress legislated in the Civil Service Reform Act that all agencies must have a performance evaluation system in place by the start of fiscal 1982. The system selected by the Department of Health and Human Services required standards of performance for all job elements and detailed three levels of achievement—'partially met,' 'fully met,' and 'exceeded.' Two additional levels—'failed to meet' and 'outstanding'—are at the bottom and top of the ratings, respectively, giving a five-tiered rating overall.

Initial reaction was predictably hostile and included my own dismay at having to identify and then measure all the tasks performed in the section. The range of concern went from supervisors' complaints about the added time necessary for sampling and review to the employees resentment at being told, in very quantitative terms, precisely what work was expected of them. Despite the misgivings, supervisors did welcome the opportunity to replace the previous evaluation categories, which were highly subjective and required ratings of rather vague concepts such as 'cooperation,' 'initiative,' and 'persistence.'

NLM's Performance Standards Development

As noted in the pitfalls section of Dr. Leach's paper, standards do take time to develop and do cost in terms of the ongoing supervisory time needed for sampling, statistics keeping, and review. Nearly six months before the starting date (none too soon), we began developing the required standards. There was an overall processing rate already in place for the section, but no rate for individual tasks.

The first step was to identify all the tasks and measure the existing rates. For example, with check-in, samples from various hours of the day and from different individuals were collected. These data were augmented by samples for the same tasks performed by professional staff. After much discussion among the supervisors, the sample data were averaged and distributed to the staff for each task in the section for which there could be a quantitative measure.

Work plans were then prepared for each member of the staff by grade. For lower-graded employees doing the bulk of the measurable tasks, this process went rather quickly; for higher-graded employees, particularly those doing developmental work, it was more difficult. Work plans for supervisory and managerial staff tend to be more narrative and descriptive than quantitative. Even they, however, can be grounded in specifics, with time, quantity, and quality measures. For example, a librarian developing tape loading might have a job element rated 'fully met' that reads: "Develops tape data load from two vendors within the next six months."

At the start of the new fiscal year in October 1982, the work plans were all signed and in effect. Within a few months some problems surfaced. Automation has been listed as a reason for standards, but in my experience automation became the solution to what seemed to be a serious problem—statistics inflation. With quantitative standards so important, we began to see what seemed like inflation in the quantities reported by a few staff members.

Relying on a reporting system from the people doing the work, we were saddled with a thorny problem—how to ensure the accuracy of the statistics. Fortunately, our inflation coincided with the implementation of an automated check-in system. As a result, machine rather than human counts became the basis of our measures. This illustrates an important factor in standards—one must have a way to ensure the accuracy of the data.

Revision of Standards

Even before the first midyear review, many of the supervisors realized that the sampling rates could not be sustained in a production environment, so some of the figures were revised downward or ranged. For example, instead of fifteen pieces per hour for check-in, the range was set at thirteen to eighteen. This experience seemed to coincide with that of many others, who found that initial standards may be set too high to be sustained in a day-to-day work situation.

Sampling schedules could not always be met. For tasks that were not always measured by the section's statistics keeping, scheduling was a problem. In the end, those supervisors who did not do sufficient sampling were the ones who had the greatest difficulty writing both the midyear and the final evaluations.

On the other hand, at times the reviewing seemed a waste. For example, supervisors have a standard calling for a review-rate of one hundred record updates per hour. This was supposedly sampled once a month, but in reality it was almost impossible to do. Fortunately, no one had to review the reviewer's review, but if carried to extremes, work standards can cause not only supervisory overhead but may lead to supervisory breakdown.

For those employees who have less quantifiable tasks, most supervisors rely on incident folders rather than formal sampling. For example, a secretary whose job element is to route incoming calls, might have an incident folder reading:

"Sept. 2: Failed to receive message about critical staff meeting."
"Oct. 7: Did a good job routing a congressional inquiry."
"Dec. 2: Complaint from lead programmer that message not relayed."
"Dec. 10: Made an extra effort to get critical message."

This might translate into an evaluation rating as: "In the last six months only failed to receive critical communications on two occasions where typically there are 5 to 10 messages a day." Incident folders are not really desirable alternatives to strictly quantitative standards, but they seem the only answer to developing some sort of objective criteria for job tasks that defy quantification.

Another problem that became apparent after one year was that many work plans were too fragmented. In the second year, many of the more disunited job elements were consolidated into one task. For example, instead of check-in, claiming, and coding new titles as three separate job elements, they were consolidated into one—processing direct receipts. In the first year it was not unusual for many individuals to have as many as eight job elements. In the second year, most had work plans with five job elements.

Defining the Stakes in Evaluation

Not mentioned in Dr. Leach's discussion but of great importance is to outline from the start what the stakes are in the performance plan. The rewards and penalties arising from job performance that exceeds or falls below the standard should be outlined from the start. In my experience, even though 'outstanding' was not defined by standard, by default it tended to be the 'walks-on-water' rating.

To everyone's dismay, we later found that quality step increases would only be given for an outstanding rating. Needless to say, the outstanding rating had to be revised to an attainable level. For both supervisors and employees it is very important to know how performance under the standards equates with personnel actions.

Another frequent complaint, not only with standards but with any evaluation system, is how to ensure that the appraisals are administered equitably throughout the organization. As Dr. Leach mentioned, reference librarians cannot be measured as quantitatively as catalog librarians. How does one develop equitable standards? In a serials department, for instance, how does one measure a secretary who may face a varying work load, compared with a checker facing a never-ending stream of mail? Don't individuals doing production tasks have a legitimate complaint about those who also serve by sitting and waiting for work?

Another complicating factor in standards development and implementation is the changing world in which librarians work. In my own section, in the last two years, our direct check-in routine went from a wholly manual to a first-generation automated system, to a second-generation automated system. Not only did the standards shift each time, but for some months during each transition the system was not fully operational. In the developmental stages, no one could even begin to determine what the standards should be in the production environment.

Too much emphasis cannot be given to the human concerns in standards implementation. Supervisors are human, just like everyone else. Personal dislikes and reactions must not be allowed to color the performance appraisal. A strictly quantitative performance standard gives both the evaluator and the evaluatee an objective measure. In effect, it becomes insurance to the evaluatee that good performance will be rewarded despite any personal disinclination.

If presented in this light, standards can be seen as something positive rather than something to elicit hostility. At the same time supervisors must remember that standards are measuring devices, not ends in themselves. A new employee whose husband is dying of an incurable cancer surely cannot be measured without some consideration of her personal problems. Objective as standards are made to seem, they cannot be divorced totally from the individuals who measure and are measured by them.

As we approach the second final evaluation period under this system, I believe both supervisors and employees feel the performance management system has been worthwhile. Rather than having to check off a box marked quantity, quality, cooperation, a rater can now say: "Your overall rate the past year has been 31.5 pieces per hour, and in 12 samples I found only 1 substantive error." These certainly are more objective criteria than just to say the employee is doing a good job. Consequently supervisors find evaluations easier to give and less confrontational than those of prior systems.

It is evident to both the evaluator and the evaluatee that the figures write the evaluation. At the same time supervisors are aware that the standards require a lot of statistics and sampling time. It is not easy to sample consistently and to keep the statistics and records needed to make a proper evaluation under the standard.

The standards can be prone to error, especially if the ratee keeps the figures. They must be constantly revised as systems change—and what system doesn't change? In the end, performance standards are just yardsticks that tell managers in a concrete way what they already know—most employees are good, a few are substandard, and a few are outstanding.

By Johanna Bowen

Dr. Leach has given an excellent overview of performance standards. I want to give a personal, anecdotal response. Three years ago, in October 1980, the state of New York introduced a new evaluation system based on performance standards. It affected some one hundred thousand members of the Civil Service Employees Association.

Workshops run by management consultants brought all the supervisors from the various state agencies together. (In this context, the State University of New York was merely another agency.) The system of setting mutually acceptable standards and goals for each job was virtually ignored during the initial training sessions; a less important factor—the rating—stole the show. The immediate supervisor and employee were to follow all the prescribed steps to arrive at mutually acceptable standards and a subsequent evaluation based on those standards. But the *rating* was to be done by a third party one step (or half a state) removed from the principals!

Even now, I object to this aspect of the evaluation process. But it is defended by the state of New York as being a "fairer" system than its predecessor because it acknowledges a hierarchical imperative. Upper-echelon managers have to be involved in evaluations at the production (of services) level. In my opinion, the ratings will, of necessity, be closely tied to the literary and verbal skills of the supervisor.

For the first year, the evaluations were required every six months. That was certainly too frequent. The current rate of one per year seems well suited to the work flow of most departments. On the plus side of things, I will state emphatically that I do not for a moment miss having to rate an employee's thoroughness, initiative, perseverance, flexibility, and judgment on a scale of 1 to 6.

Jobs evolve, and so do the people who hold those jobs. An automated serials control system will call for new skills and responsibilities that can easily be added to the tasks and standards. The New York State Office of Employee Relations finds the primary objection raised at this point is that the implementation of performance standards is too time-consuming.

I am convinced that the time spent in articulating standards for accomplishing the goals of a unit within the broader service framework of a functioning library is time well spent. It is true that separate performance standards must be developed for each employee or each class of similar positions and these individualized standards must be clearly linked to the goals of the library.

As librarians attempt to do more and more with fewer and fewer resources, they can all too easily find themselves unable to articulate any goal more complex than "keeping the doors open ninety hours a week" or just "doing the job." Working within the framework of performance standards can help provide an environment in which librarians do think about and articulate the goals of the library.

TECHNICAL BIBLIOGRAPHIC STANDARDS DEVELOPMENT IN THE UNITED STATES

By Robert S. Tannehill, Jr.

What is the American National Standards Institute (ANSI)? Located in New York City and founded in 1918, ANSI is a not-for-profit organization that (1) coordinates the voluntary development of national consensus standards by ANSI-accredited organizations or ANSI-organized bodies (i.e., committees), (2) provides and administers the only system recognized in the U.S. for establishing American National Standards (the system includes mechanisms for the identification of needed standards, approval procedures, timely development of standards, and recognition/ publicity of standards), and (3) provides U.S. representation in international standards bodies (e.g., the International Organization for Standardization [ISO]).

The ANSI body most relevant to the overall information community is American National Standards Committee Z39, which develops four types of standards related to library and information science and publishing:

- OFFICIAL (developed and promulgated under the procedures and policies of the American National Standards Institute)
- TECHNICAL (deal with formats, codes, constructs, transliteration schemes, and so forth, as opposed to guidelines or standards for collection development, library space, cataloging rules, etc.)
- VOLUNTARY (use not required by ANSI. They could, however, be required under systems or networks that have adopted an ANSI standard)
- CONSENSUS (developed and approved by broad information industry representation, where "information" is used in its broadest

sense, encompassing the library community, publishing, information services, and so on)

Z39 has been incorporated as a not-for-profit entity and is in the process
of shifting from an ANSI committee to an ANSI-accredited organization,
which will reduce bureaucratic levels and speed up the standards approval process. Z39 even plans to change its name so it will be more
readily identifiable as a national information standards organization
(rather than a fighter plane or a vitamin), but until that process is final,
the name remains ANSC Z39.

Z39: Specifics

Z39 publishes a brochure that lists the approximately forty American
National Standards it has developed over the forty-four years of its
existence. This would appear to be about one new standard per year,
but in reality there has been much more activity over the past ten years
than in the preceding thirty-four. A few of the most important standards
include:

ISO EQUIVALENT	ANSI DESIGNATION	NAME OF STANDARD
ISO-2709	Z39.2	Bibliographic Interchange on Magnetic Tape [the basis for the MARC communication format]
ISO-4	Z39.5	The Abbreviation of Titles of Publications
ISO-3297	Z39.9	Identification Number for Serial Publications [ISSN]
ISO-2108	Z39.21	Book Numbering [ISBN]
ISO-3166	Z39.27	Structure for the Representation of Names of Countries
ISO-690	Z39.29	Bibliographic References
*	Z39.30	Order Form for Single Titles of Library Materials
*	Z39.42	Serial Holdings at the Summary Level
*	Z39.43	Identification Code for the Book Industry [SAN]

* = No ISO equivalent standard.

It may not be generally understood that not only does Z39 develop new standards but, at least every five years, it reviews the existing ones. Then, members of the committee, who represent the many facets of the information community, either reaffirm the existing standards, revise or update them, or, if they are no longer viable, drop them.

The development of ANSI standards is an interesting process, particularly if one is on a Z39 subcommittee. Z39 standards have shifted over the years from those that are primarily "print or manual process"-oriented to those with computer applications as their main thrust. Thus, one notes such recent standards as:

NAME OF STANDARD	ANSI DESIGNATION
Bibliographic Information Interchange on Magnetic Tape	Z39.2
International Standard Serial Numbering (ISSN)	Z39.9
Book Numbering (ISBN)	Z39.21
Structure for the Representation of Names of Countries of the World for Information Processing	Z39.27
Identification Code for the Book Industry (SAN)	Z39.43

This trend is also evident in the work in progress in the Z39 subcommittees. Examples of the twenty-three draft standards are:

NAME OF DRAFT STANDARD	Z39 SUBCOMMITTEE
Computer-Related	
Computer-to-Computer Protocol	D
Bibliographic Data File Identification	J
Coded Character Sets for Bibliographic Information Interchange	N
Standard Format for Computerized Book Ordering	U
Examples of Other Standards in Process	
Standard Order Form for the Purchase of Multiple Titles	T
Language Codes	C
Romanization of Yiddish	5
Environmental Conditions for Storage of Paper-based Library Materials	R
Permanent Paper for Printed Library Materials	S

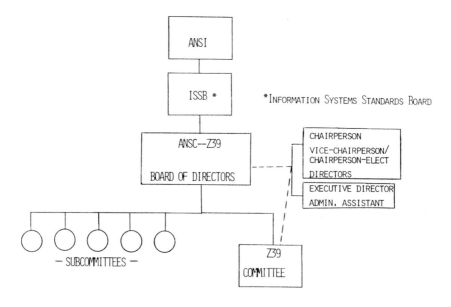

American National Standards Committee Z39 Organization.

Z39's extensive activity requires lean, efficient organization, and it has such through its board of directors, its membership, and its subcommittees—all coordinated by an executive director. The Z39 membership is highly active and important, for it votes on new areas to be standardized and comments on and approves new draft standards.

The subcommittees develop all new standards—whether created from "scratch" (based on the recommendations of librarians, data base vendors, computer programmers in the information field, linguists, publishers, and so on) or whether existing *de facto* standards are adopted and processed through the Z39/ANSI procedures and work flow. For example, Z39 Subcommittee AA is currently working on an interlibrary loan form standard based on the ALA ILL form.

The basic standards development process is:

Recommendation——>Approval——>Subcommittee——>Draft————>Draft ———>
                 by Z39   appointed   standard   reviewed
                 membership   developed   by Z39
                                                            membership
                                                            for comment

Draft voted on by————>ANSI ——>Public ———>Final ———>American
Z39 membership   ISSB   comment   ANSI   National
(approval)   approval   approval   Standard

This process may take as little as one year, or it may take several years, depending on the complexity of the standard and how well entrenched are the "other ways" of performing the function being standardized (e.g., the bibliographic references standard).

Voice of Z39

In addition to its brochure, Z39 also publishes the *Voice of Z39*, a quarterly newsletter that keeps readers current on published standards as well as new standards being developed. Z39 members receive the *Voice* as part of their membership. Many libraries subscribe to the *Voice* to keep abreast of U.S. standardization activities.

Z39 has two levels of membership—full, voting members and informational members. The latter cannot vote or hold office, but they do receive Z39 mailings, including the *Voice of Z39*. As of November 1983, Z39 had forty-three full members and eighty-one informational members. Information on membership can be obtained from Patricia Harris, Executive Director of Z39, at the following address:

> ANSC Z39
> c/o National Bureau of Standards
> Library, Room E106
> Washington, DC 20234

In each copy of the *Voice* is a form on which the reader may send Z39 his or her recommendations for areas in which standards are needed. Readers may photocopy the form and submit multiple requests, as well as distribute copies to their colleagues. Merely send the recommendations to the Z39 office, and they will be given a careful review. Keep in mind that the *Voice of Z39* informs the reader of new areas of standardization that are in process.

To summarize, ANSC Z39 develops technical, official, voluntary, and consensus standards related to library and information science and publishing. It is an active, responsive organization that continues to provide important standards—standards critical to the effective, efficient development of the U.S. library and information community. The interest, participation, and recommendations of the library community are welcome.

UNIFORMITY IN UNION LISTS OF SERIALS: MEASURING UP TO STANDARDS

By Marjorie E. Bloss

The individual confronted for the first time with the editorial responsibility for a union list of serials may feel somewhat akin to the Children
of Israel as they awaited Moses' descent from Mount Sinai. There is
apprehension. There is anticipation. There is even a parallel to the two
stone tablets on which the commandments were inscribed. In the case
of a union list of serials, these tablets are the rules governing the bibliographic description of a title and those dictating the construction of
holdings statements.

Once these "commandments" for creating a union list of serials are
examined more closely, one discovers with some dismay that further
interpretations of the rules, and decisions about their application, are
essential. Like the Ten Commandments, the *Anglo-American Cataloguing
Rules*, 2nd edition (*AACR2*) and the *American National Standard for Serial
Holdings Statements at the Summary Level* (here abbreviated as the ANSI
Standard for Serial Holdings Statements) are the framework within which
union list editors must operate.

They don't always identify the variations one may encounter or give
guidance on how to handle every situation. Often interpretations are
left to the individual, who may feel frustrated and uncertain at having
to make an independent decision. These feelings are especially intense
when dealing with standards. Unconsciously, librarians come to a standard (or a *de facto* one) with the impression that it is going to answer all
their questions. This is certainly not the case with either *AACR2* or the
ANSI *Standard for Serial Holdings Statements*. In many instances, guidance
is altogether lacking.

As in many areas of the library profession, the development of union listing is evolutionary, and the final word on the topic has not yet been uttered. Here I want to identify some of the major issues confronting union list editors who attempt to apply these standards and rules. Perhaps by discussing some of the grey areas it will become apparent that standards are pertinent to the majority of union lists and that almost everyone responsible for a union list of serials will have to confront the same issues at one time or another. I will focus on the bibliographic data and the holdings statement used in a union list rather than on the MARC formats developed for them. In no way do I underestimate the importance of the MARC formats, for they provide a flexibility not previously possible for manipulating data. Yet I am primarily concerned with the form of the data the user of a union list will ultimately need. I will also report on some recent developments in the area of union list standards that will further influence library work.

Bibliographic Data and Union Lists: Tradition

Like peanut butter and jelly or Laurel and Hardy, the listing of a serial title and the holdings statements in it are, for union list purposes, an inseparable team. An identification number such as an ISSN (International Standard Serial Number) can be used to represent a title, but traditionally some bibliographic description of the title has been used. The major questions and issues here are how many bibliographic data are appropriate for a union list of serials record, and what standards have been or are currently applicable to the selection of the data elements.

For many years, the five-volume *Union List of Serials in the United States and Canada (ULS)* and its successor, *New Serial Titles (NST)*, were regarded as the epitome of a union list of serials bibliographic record. Included in this record were main entry, title (if different from main entry), beginning and ending dates (if known and/or applicable), publication/distribution information, series, linking entries and notes concerning numbering irregularities and suspensions. Other notes were omitted, as were subject headings and added entries. The arrangement of these union lists was strictly by main entry, with an occasional cross-reference thrown in. For the most part, however, if the main entry or its exact form were not known, finding a particular title could be a major problem.

As seen in both the *Union List of Serials in the United States and Canada* and *New Serial Titles*, the bibliographic data used for union listing were obviously a subset of the fuller cataloging record. While there were many years of tradition on which to base the content of the bibliographic data in these sources, there was nothing that could formally have been declared a standard. For those compiling other union lists, little concrete guidance was available, except by example.

In late 1980, there was a change in the amount of information contained in the bibliographic records of *NST*. Due to a change from the manual to the machine-derived method of compiling *NST*, the new union list of serials record became, in many cases, identical to a full cataloging record. As full a bibliographic record as appears on the machine-readable tape at the time of compilation is included in *NST*. More detailed notes and subject and added entry tracings are currently part of the record as well as those data elements listed before. Does this then imply that the bibliographic data for a union list of serials record should now include the same data elements as a cataloging record?

If this were not enough to raise the level of confusion, *AACR2* came along at about the same time with not just one but three levels of bibliographic description. Unfortunately, the choice of which standards to use was left up to the individual. The Library of Congress, for instance, has opted to use an "augmented Level One" for the bibliographic description of serials for cataloging purposes. As with earlier cataloging codes, however, there is nothing in *AACR2* that specifically spells out those data elements essential to a union list of serials bibliographic record.

Bibliographic Data and Union Lists: Evolving Trends

Faced with these nonanswers, where is the editor of a union list of serials to turn for advice and guidance? To begin with, he or she must ask some basic questions about the list itself. What is its purpose? If it is to be used primarily as a finding tool rather than for cataloging, one might argue that fewer bibliographic data are needed. But if the time ever came when a more complete record were desired, some method of adding data elements would be required. In many cases, a considerable amount of time and energy would have to be expended to accomplish this augmentation. Perhaps the axiom here should be: "Better too much than too little."

The size of the union list of serials may also determine the number of bibliographic data included. If the list is large and funds are scarce, a limited number of data might be selected for inclusion. On the other hand, the larger the list, the greater the chance of identical titles (the usual favorites like *Annual Report*, *Bulletin*, and *Publication* come to mind) appearing. As a result, some mechanism—such as key title, uniform title, place of publication, or even publisher—is needed to distinguish between publications, thus increasing the number of data. Furthermore,

I am convinced large lists require more bibliographic data than smaller ones; those who contribute to them as well as those who use them are generally bibliographically sophisticated.

A number of union lists of serials compiled today use the machine-readable CONSER file available online through OCLC. When a bibliographic record is selected for a union list, as full a record as resides in the database is earmarked for that list. At the time of production, the editor of the union list can select those data elements deemed necessary. The result may be a very abbreviated entry or one containing the full cataloging record.

As with the bibliographic record found in the *Union List of Serials in the United States and Canada* and the "old" *NST*, the union list record extracted from magnetic tapes can also be viewed as a subset of the full cataloging record. Unlike the earlier union list record, however, librarians now have the ability to extract the pieces of information they want from a more complete cataloging record.

In addition, the parent record remains eminently accessible, and the union list editor can select or omit other data at will. The flexibility editors now have when choosing the bibliographic data elements of union lists is so great that the question of what constitutes a union list of serials bibliographic record is no longer the major concern it once was; the computerized manipulation of data has almost made it a moot point.

Basic Union List Bibliographic Record

It is easy to dismiss this entire problem by simply advising librarians to connect to the online CONSER file, or to keep adding or deleting data elements in their computer-derived offline products until they get it right. Even if the former is feasible, the latter is going to cost in reprogramming charges every time the librarian changes his or her mind. Furthermore, some lists will still be created manually. I am, therefore, here proposing what I consider to be the basic elements for a union list of serials bibliographic record:

1. Main entry
2. Title (if different from main entry)
3. Uniform title (to distinguish between two identical titles)
4. Edition statement
5. Numeric/chronological designations
6. Place of publication/distribution
7. Publisher/distributor

8. Notes, especially if they deal with:
    a. Other title information
    b. Numbering irregularities
    c. Other physical formats
    d. Linking entry information that indicates the relationship of the serial with its preceding or succeeding entries
    e. ISSN and Key Title
    f. Any control or bibliographic numbers

It is true that the above elements and fields lean more toward a full cataloging record than the earlier abbreviated union list of serials record. Yet I believe the fields cited are essential to basic knowledge about a title and are not merely extraneous pieces of information occupying valuable space. The inclusion of these data elements is further supported by the American Library Association's Ad Hoc Committee on Union Lists of Serials' *Guidelines for Union Lists of Serials*.[1] It is also supported by the work Jean Whiffin has done for the IFLA/UNESCO project on union catalogs of serials.[2]

To the question, "Is anything being done to establish these or other sets of data elements as a standard for a union list of serials bibliographic record?" the answer is, "Not really." To my knowledge no work on this problem is being done in the United States.

On the international front, however, Ms. Whiffin's recommendations for a union list of serials bibliographic record are being evaluated by the International Federation of Library Associations and Institutions' (IFLA's) Section on Serial Publications. By 1984, this committee (probably) will establish general guidelines for a basic union list of serials record. It is doubtful, however, that a formal standard will be created. Because of the increased usage of online serial files and the facility with which the data in them can be manipulated, the need for a standard has diminished greatly.

The ANSI Standard

The holdings statement (i.e., an indication of the specific volumes and/or years of a serial retained by a library) is the second but coequal component of a union list of serials. As they had for the content of the bibliographic data, the *Union List of Serials in the United States and Canada* and *NST* served for many years as the unofficial standard for holdings statements.

As with the bibliographic description for a union list record, the procedures for establishing concrete guidelines for holdings statements were amazingly similar. For the most part one followed by example, leaving a fair amount to implication and the rest to imagination. Fortunately, in most cases imaginations ran in similar patterns. This was especially true with regard to uniformity in the use of punctuation in a holdings statement. There were many other instances, however, when questions arose in the "but-what-do-we-do-when" category. In these cases, there were no definitive answers.

The CONSER Project has been credited with a number of accomplishments, among them, pointing out that some mechanism for the standardization of serial holdings statements was sorely needed. The result was the American National Standards Institute's (ANSI's) Subcommittee Z39.40, which formed in 1975 for the purpose of defining serial holdings statements at the summary level. After eight drafts, the *Standard* was at long last approved for use by the library community. Unlike any previous document, this one was written with union lists of serials in mind.[3]

The creation of standards is done with a combination of practical experience and idealistic expectations. While the intentions of the authors are almost always good, there is no way that all situations and ramifications of the rules can be predicted. Perhaps even more significant is that standards are in most cases the work of two or more people. Differences of opinion are bound to occur.

ANSI standards, regardless of subject, must be approved by the voting members of that particular section. While unanimity is not essential, serious attempts must be made to reconcile opposing points of view. Compromise, of course, comes into play whenever one attempts to resolve conflicting positions. The result is that standards are compromises, not the embodiment of the single, consistent vision one often expects.

Even on this sobering note of reality, it should be emphasized that compromises can be either good or bad. How successful were the negotiations on this particular standard?

As one who has coded many thousands of holdings statements according to the ANSI *Standard for Serial Holdings Statements at the Summary Level*, I am pleased to say that in the vast majority of cases, there is little trouble in applying it. Although redundant when reporting the *Standard*'s Third Level (i.e., enumeration and chronology), the coding for the completeness, acquisitions, and nonretention codes becomes automatic fairly quickly. The punctuation prescribed in the *Standard* is functional and sufficiently limited so that a user does not have to rely continually on little charts or "help" screens.

Even so, heavy users of the *Standard* have encountered situations covered either vaguely or not at all. I need not elaborate on the *Standard*'s inconclusive rules about when to apply second-order enumeration and chronology, when to have enumeration and chronology correlate, and the problems created by the rule prohibiting captions. While a certain amount of flexibility in a standard is permissible and even desirable, too much leeway results in insufficient uniformity, thus negating the standard's purpose.

To ameliorate this situation, OCLC has recently published a manual that attempts to "standardize" the *Standard*. This manual, *Serial Holdings Statements at the Summary Level: User Guide to the American National Standard*,[4] discusses the various interpretive possibilities of the *Standard* and indicates preferences. Though the *User Guide* is geared to OCLC users, I believe it has value for members of other utilities and for compilers of manual union lists as well. It is available to both OCLC and non-OCLC users.

A New Standard for Serial Holdings Statements

Soon after the ANSI *Standard for Serial Holdings Statements at the Summary Level* was approved, ANSI began to work on a similar standard for detailed (i.e., copy-specific) holdings statements. The draft of this proposed standard ran into problems when it was distributed for a vote.

The negative comments focused on the fact that there were some basic differences between the draft standard and the final one. These differences included the order of enumeration and chronology; whether or not to include captions; the treatment of different physical formats for the same title; and some mechanism for designating alternative numbering schemes. Of even more concern was whether to have two standards for holdings statements or to consolidate them.

The method chosen to resolve these differences was a 2½-day work-session at Airlie House, Virginia, supported by the Council on Library Resources. Invited were the committee members who had worked on the ANSI *Summary Standard* and the draft *Detailed Standard*. A group of observers who for various reasons had a vested interest in the outcome was also invited. Representation in this group included individuals from ANSC Z39 itself, OCLC (whose members probably constitute the most numerous users of the *Summary Standard*), the Southeastern ARL Libraries Cooperative Serials Project (developers of the *MARC Format for Holdings Statements*), and IFLA (whose Section on Serial Publications I represented). A professional facilitator was on hand to keep the situation on an even keel and to lend an objective point of view when members took to their various soap boxes.

The success of the work-sessions exceeded the hopes of all who attended. The group unanimously recommended that a single standard on serial holdings statements, incorporating both the detailed and summary standards, be developed. And the new responsibility was given to the Detailed Holdings Standard Committee (Subcommittee E of ANSC Z39) to begin work on the composite standard. These recommendations were subsequently approved by ballot of the voting members and alternates of ANSC Z39. Included in the resolved issues on the content of the new standard itself are the following:

1. The order of enumeration and chronology data will conform to that found in ISBD(S) (i.e., enumeration followed immediately in parenthesis by its related chronological data).
2. The inclusion of captions if they are available for summary holdings; mandatory inclusion for detailed holdings.
3. Though the preference for the treatment of different physical formats is to use separate bibliographic records for each, if an institution decides to use one bibliographic record for all formats, then separate strings of data would have to be created for each format.
4. Square brackets would be employed in a holdings statement to indicate alternative numbering schemes.

A new, single standard for serial holdings statements (both summary and detailed) will be sent to ANSC Z39's voting members. Assuming this new draft standard is accepted, a motion will then be made to withdraw the *Summary Holdings Standard*. Quite understandably, a fair amount of concern has been expressed by those who have coded thousands of holdings statements according to the *Summary Standard*. How will the changes affect previously coded holdings statements? Will it be necessary to go back and redo all the earlier work? The answer emphatically is *no*. A "grandfather" clause will be built in (at least for OCLC users), permitting those holdings statements based on the *Summary Standard* to remain. It will probably be recommended that a holdings statement requiring some alteration be modified to reflect the new standard. All *new* holdings statements should, of course, be formatted according to the new standard.

Serial Holdings Statements Internationally

In addition to the work being done in this country on holdings statements, a project is underway on an international scale. This one is under the auspices of the IFLA Section on Serial Publications. The project's purpose is to form the basis for an ISO (International Standards Organization) standard on serial holdings statements.

As a participant, I have analyzed the national library practices and standards of thirty-eight countries with regard to punctuation and internal guidelines. I have compared them in hopes of detecting similar patterns in the way specific functions are handled (such as the order of enumeration and chronology, gaps in holdings, the use of captions, etc.).

One very interesting trend that has surfaced is the emphasis placed on ISBD(S) by national libraries developing (or planning to develop) standards on holdings statements. This surprises me because I had never viewed ISBD(S) as a vehicle for holdings information. Because of the high regard placed on it by responding libraries, ISBD(S) will form the basic framework for my recommendations.

Once the prescribed punctuation and some basic principles for formatting holdings statements are submitted to, and approved by, the Section on Serial Publications, these recommendations will be forwarded to ISO. This group in turn will determine if the recommended measures are appropriate to serve as the basis for a standard on serial holdings statements.

I have discussed the background of U.S. union list traditions and given an overview of the standards (or lack of them) in current use. Some comments on the work being done on potential standards that might affect union lists in the future have also been offered.

My experience suggests that no standard will ever fulfill the ideal of providing an eternal answer to every situation. On the other hand, the library standard that provides a solid framework for uniformity is a major step toward the sharing of information and resources.

References

1. Marjorie E. Bloss et al., *Guidelines for Union Lists of Serials* (Chicago: American Library Association, Resources and Technical Services Division, 1982), p. 19.

2. Jean Whiffin, *Guidelines for Union Catalogues of Serials* (first draft prepared for the IFLA Section on Serial Publications, Victoria, B.C., 1981), p. 23.

3. American National Standards Institute, *American National Standard for Serial*

Holdings Statements at the Summary Level (New York: American National Standards Institute, 1980), foreword.

4. OCLC Union List Standard Task Force, *Serial Holdings Statements at the Summary Level: User Guide to the American National Standard* (Dublin, Ohio: OCLC, 1983).

STANDARDS AND SERIALS: MEANINGFUL RELATIONSHIPS

By Linda K. Bartley

I have chosen "meaningful relationships" as the theme of this paper. What is particularly exciting about standards and serials right now is that at last so much of what librarians have been working toward has, or is about to, come to pass. Many pieces of the puzzle have been developed, and now is the time to figure out how they join together. Each standard has merit, but librarianship is on the brink of realizing the payoff from their intermingling, their meaningful relationships! For example, the newly published Z39 serials claim form explicitly draws on six other standards. Standards beget standards.

A particularly impressive recent development was the preparation of the MARC Holdings and Locations Format. It draws on the MARC format in general and two Z39 standards—those for expressing holdings at the detailed and at the summary levels—that, happily, have become interrelated. (By the way, it is refreshing to note that serials served as trailblazers for the other formats—the idea being that if serial holdings could be described sufficiently for machine manipulation, nonserial materials would be a piece of cake.) The MARC Holdings and Locations Format has received MARBI's tentative approval, and a group instrumental in its development—the Southeastern ARL Libraries Cooperative Serials Project—is putting it to the test.

For some time now, librarians have been rightfully preoccupied with the form and content of serials cataloging records—this very much in response to the need to master AACR2. As the newness of the retooling wanes, they are turning their attention to conversion projects, union listing, book catalogs, and other things that make the whole greater than the sum of its parts. They are beginning to pay more attention to the reasons why those records were built in the first place.

The following is an outline of four standards/serials relationships I shall describe in some detail, all of which involve "real-life" applications of standards or standardized practices in the realm of serials:

1. CONSER (CONversion of SERials) authentication and self-authentication = relationships of participants in a cooperative project; relationships among the data in the 042 field insofar as they are indications of the completeness of cataloging records.
2. Linking entry fields = the chronological relationship of serials.
3. U.S. Newspaper Program and the single-record technique = relationship of different physical manifestations of the same item.
4. The CONSER Abstracting & Indexing Project = the relationships of information communities with common needs.

Authentication and Self-Authentication

A CONSER participants meeting and a CONSER operational staff meeting were held back to back on September 22 and 23, 1983. In preparation for the meetings, we at LC developed a proposal that addressed what had become a chronic problem: our inability to keep up with the authentication workload. The authentication process essentially consists of confirming the accuracy of description, name authorities, and content designation. We incorporated in our proposal the idea of delegating authentication to those CONSER institutions deemed "independent" (i.e., those that have passed a quality review). The quality of even the independent institutions' records would continue to be monitored with sampling procedures; authentication would continue as usual for those institutions whose quality review had not been completed.

We further proposed that certain codes now defined for use in the 042 field (which indicates level of authentication) be retired and that two other codes now in use be redefined in a way that would expand their usefulness while not negating their past meaning. Specifically, the code "msc" would be redefined to denote minimal-level authentication, and the code "lcd" would be redefined to denote the presence of authority work for all name headings in a given record. If LC encounters one of these "lcd" or "msc" records in the course of its current cataloging, the code will be changed to "lc." Furthermore, we intend to authenticate the records for all surrogates now on hand.

The participants greeted the notion of self-authentication (and all that it implies) with real enthusiasm. The ensuing discussion resulted in an embellishment of LC's proposal. It drew on considerations of name authorities and minimal-level cataloging. Under the new scheme, an independent NACO institution, which normally would authenticate at the "lcd" level, might enter minimal-level records authenticated as "msc." Conversely, an independent non-NACO institution, which would normally authenticate at the "msc" level, would enter "lcd" in the 042 field if authoritative forms of name—for *all* names in a given record—were found in LC's name-authority file (as maintained on OCLC). Instructions on how to perform self-authentication will be developed by LC, taking into account such matters as the need to input/modify LC card numbers, what values are appropriate for the encoding level, and what kinds of modification requests would still need to be submitted to LC in writing. LC will also develop guidelines for determining when a record originally entered as "minimal" has been updated to the extent that it is no longer "minimal."

This new direction is particularly exciting, for it takes better advantage of the common expertise developed in the CONSER project. It will allow for a more explicit indication of how a given record is evolving against record-completeness and name-authority expectations. The guidelines for standardized practice on this account are, among others, the *National Level Bibliographic Record—Serials* and authoritative forms of names established in accordance with LC's interpretation of AACR2.

Linking Entry Fields

To talk about linking entry fields implies that a decision has already been made that a title change has taken place. Increasingly, catalogers attend to the parameters of a record, the choice of a record with the correct "span" in certain ways being more important than the perfection of the contents of that very record.

AACR2 caused enormous problems. Those who deal with serials could not close the catalog. Catalogers are still reeling from the effort to conjoin and rework records created under different rules. In CONSER we are making a diligent effort at least to identify those cases where records created under different rules cannot coexist (mostly, we suspect, where there is not a one-to-one relationship in terms of entry.)

In another matter affecting links, a revised LC rule interpretation has been issued. It sets out the various combinations of main entry, title, and edition that should be given in the linking entry. Coincidentally, new subfield codes in the MARC format have been defined, specifying, for example, that the main-entry uniform-title heading (130 in the parent record) should be given in subfield ≠ a in the linking entry. In any event, the CONSER documentation will be revised to reflect the outcome of how serials are to be cited.

U.S. Newspaper Program

The Library of Congress is actively involved in the U.S. Newspaper Program (USNP) at two levels. First, the Serial & Government Publications Division has been involved in the program from its inception and, as a special CONSER member, is one of the seven national repositories now cooperatively building the database. At the second level, the Serial Record Division is providing technical management and documentation support to the program, as well as coordination between the program and CONSER. It is in the latter role that LC librarians have taken an interest in a bibliographic approach to handling differing physical formats. The approach has to do with the U.S. Newspaper Project's being as much a cataloging as a union list project.

To talk about newspapers is to talk about microfilm and often multiple microfilmers of a given title. There will be in excess of 450,000 unique titles identified in the USNP. To have multiple records for each of them seemed regrettable *and*, after a bit of thought, avoidable. The practice to be followed in the project will be to catalog a title *once*, i.e., to create a master bibliographic record for the publication as originally issued. To this master will be appended local-data records (LDRs) for all the forms in which a given institution holds the title. There will be a separate LDR for each type of physical format, e.g., original, microfilm, microfiche, etc. In the local-data record for the microfilm holdings, the microproducer will be represented by an NUC (National Union Catalog) code, and a code will be used to express if the copy is service, master, or preservation master. Also, the span of dates will be given.

This is a more orderly way of dealing with a wealth of compatible but competing information that would be extremely difficult to decipher if it were presented in separate bibliographic records. With this technique the collating is done at the outset, making the chronology of holdings hang together. Perhaps the implementation of the MARC Holdings and Locations Format will permit it to be extended to all types of serials as well as other bibliographic materials.

CONSER Abstracting and Indexing Project

Real progress has been made toward the implementation of a project, cosponsored by the Association of Research Libraries and the National Federation of Abstracting and Information Services, to secure the systematic addition of abstracting and indexing information in the 510 field in CONSER records. Funds—enough to handle the posting of over 105,000 citations spread across roughly half as many unique serial titles—have been obtained from several sources.

A&I information has been variously added to CONSER records over the years. One of the thrusts of Abstracting and Indexing Project, however, is to make such additions consistently, drawing on the cooperation of the A&I service to supply and perpetually maintain their accuracy. A description of some of the benefits likely to be derived from the project underscores the payoffs from the use of standards and standardized processes. The benefits include:

- the introduction of needed links between the A&I services' citations and the library records through standardization of A&I serials title citations into the forms found in library catalogs;
- learning which A&I services cover a given serial; and
- an improved ability to identify and locate serials cited by A&I services because of the presence of records for the cited serials in the CONSER database.

As a result of the project, librarians will have access to up-to-date information about the extent to which serials are covered by abstracting and indexing services. Such A&I "union list" information is needed for reference and interlibrary loan purposes. In the area of acquisitions, the enriched and expanded CONSER database will help librarians make decisions on new subscriptions, cancellations, binding and retention, and whether or not to rely on resource sharing in lieu of ownership.

Given all the above, I would venture that standards and serials are indeed having a meaningful, *ongoing* relationship. Whether it will get them down the aisle remains to be seen!

TRENDS IN THE MARKETING OF SERIALS TO LIBRARIES

By Patricia E. Sabosik

The H. W. Wilson Company is a leading publisher of periodical and book indexes and reference books, a database producer, and soon to be a database vendor. Its periodical and book indexes are serially published. The indexing deals primarily with periodical literature. It ranges from the general, such as *Reader's Guide to Periodical Literature*, to the specific, such as *Index to Legal Periodicals, Art Index*, and *Biography Index*.

Wilson has been publishing monographs and indexes since the turn of the century, and its primary market continues to be libraries. A few examples in this paper will illustrate how Wilson markets serials to libraries. I shall draw on my experience in publishing (on the editorial *and* marketing sides) to present, from a publisher's point of view, comments on marketing serials to libraries.

First I shall discuss the marketing concept, then the library market. Interwoven will be a discussion of serials publishing trends as they have developed, along with an explanation of why they developed.

The Marketing Concept

In defining the concept of marketing, I draw my ideas from Peter Drucker, a management consultant and author, and Philip Kotler, professor at Northwestern University School of Management. Drucker states: "Marketing is so basic that it cannot be considered a separate function of a business.... It is the whole business seen from the point of view of its final result, that is, from the customer's point of view."[1] From him one sees that marketing means customer awareness and sensitivity.

Kotler continues the explanation:

> Marketing has evolved from its early origins in selling and distribution into a comprehensive philosophy for relating an organization dynamically to its markets. It is the study of exchange processes and relationships, and has its origins in economics. The marketing concept deals with the way a company, or institution, looks at their relations with their customers or publics.[2]

The key word here is *customer*. The library market, any market, is made up of *people* with money to spend; focusing on the customer, therefore, is the marketing objective. The economic thread that runs through marketing is strong also. Many of the business situations and trends I cite here are reactions to economic factors, from inflation and unemployment to general consumer confidence in products and services.

In the early years of modern business (circa 1920s/30s), firms were primarily production-oriented due to the great demand for products relative to available supplies. In the 1950s, particularly for manufacturing firms but also for publishers, there was little need to stimulate demand, and companies used their time and resources to develop more efficient methods of generating greater output.

Later, as competition and supply expanded, the need to identify and penetrate available markets became mandatory for long-term survival. The same has been true in the publishing industry. Business began shifting its emphasis from products to customers. That's what marketing is essentially all about.

In the publishing industry, serials are defined as manufactured products and librarians as a customer group. What leads companies to discover marketing? Kotler has identified five issues:[3]

1. *Sales Decline*
   A firm is in business to make a profit. A percentage of profits is reinvested in the business for research and development or capital expenditures for new equipment to keep the business up to date and functional. Sales decline could be caused by a number of factors, but customers are the most immediate area of consideration.

   For some publishers today, sales are declining in the grades K-12 school market due to demographic shifts. As a result they are looking for different customers to buy their products. Two growth areas identified by the publishing industry are the business and professional book market and special libraries not dependent on federal funding.

2. *Slow Growth*

If business is not growing, the firm may look at its customer base for an explanation. Demographics may be the cause. Or perhaps the product is maturing and nearing the end of its "life cycle" (obsolescence). When it is no longer economically justifiable for a publisher to continue issuing a series, set, or periodical, it is discontinued.

To counteract slow growth, a publisher may look to another type of market or a new industry. Television created a world of new characters that juvenile publishers and agents latched onto in a licensing frenzy (an example of product-oriented marketing), and the acquisitions librarian is faced with the problem of choosing juvenile series with *some* literary merit.

3. *Changing Buying Patterns*

The way customers buy products may be affected by demographic or economic shifts, or both. According to Book Industry statistics, acquisitions for public school libraries showed a decrease in the number of *books* purchased over the period 1980 to 1982 from 56.3 million to 54.03 million units, a total decrease of 2.27 million units. There was an increase, however, in the number of *periodicals* purchased over the same period, from 1.6 million in 1980 to 1.63 million in 1982, an increase of 300,000 units.[4] This shift clearly indicates that schools are buying fewer books and more periodicals for their library collections.

4. *Increasing Sales Expenditures*

If a firm's sales costs are increasing at so high a rate as to cut too far into profits, the company will look for new markets to expand sales (thereby keeping costs and prices down) or discontinue the product. With the objective of expanding circulation and controlling costs, journal publishers who market to research institutions will also market to professionals in the field.

5. *Increasing Competition*

With few true monopolies in American business, a firm facing any or all of the above issues is not alone. Publishers compete for a share of the library market, and their competition often takes the form of differentiation of new products or services, the emphasis usually on services. The following quotation from Jennifer Cargill illustrates this point:

In order to grow, both the old and new companies must continue to compete for the business of a relatively constant group of library customers. In many cases, the only way for one firm to expand and survive is by taking customers away from a competitor.... Book jobbers, whether domestic or foreign, all sell the same books, with the exception of those who specialize in a subject or category.... In essence, Ambassador, Baker & Taylor, Ballen, B. H. Blackwell, Blackwell North America, Coutts, Book House, Harrassowitz, Nihoff, and others market the same products and compete for the same customer group. Similarly, Faxon, EBSCO, Swets, and their competitors sell the same basic group of periodicals, and continuations. How do they remain competitive when they are all offering virtually the same products?[5]

The answer is *service*, the distinguishing factor.

The H. W. Wilson Company developed fourteen of its seventeen periodical and book indexes prior to 1940. Most of Wilson's major competitors came into the library market with competing indexes in the last fifteen years. One explanation is demographics, the shifting information needs of a student population as it rippled through high school, college, graduate school, and professional practice. The introduction of competing indexes into the library market has caused Wilson to reassess its marketing and selling strategies.

These are some of the reasons why a business or institution turns to marketing. Next is the implementation stage, where the marketing process, which is customer-oriented, is integrated into the firm's operation. Implementation is an evolutionary process. Kotler has identified the five developmental stages most firms pass through:

1. Marketing is advertising, sales, promotion, publicity.
2. Marketing is trying to please the customer, the introduction of benefit-selling.
3. Marketing is innovation, developing a competitive lead.
4. Marketing is positioning, finding a basis for distinguishing a product from the competition.
5. Finally, marketing is analysis, planning, and control.[6]

The following illustrate the implementation process and speculate about where specific firms and the overall publishing industry are today:

1. *Marketing is advertising, sales, and promotion.*
   This process is product-oriented. Each function is part of the overall marketing process. The influx of computer books and journals into the market today is an example of a product-oriented program. The customer is not the focal point of the book; rather, emphasis is placed on the hardware and software, the expansion of series or

the creation of new ones, and the development of a wide range of new technology journals.

2. *Marketing is benefit-selling.*

   The growing subscription agencies in the 1960s used this method of marketing to sell their services. Agencies, book jobbers, and periodical publishers (to some extent) still use it today, though it is not the focal point of their marketing programs. Benefit determination is usually coupled with product and market analysis.

3. *Marketing is innovation.*

   Innovation is a competitive strategy that differentiates one firm from a similar one in the same market. It is used to increase customers and sales. Computerization, an operations innovation, evolves as a necessary cost-cutting measure that can greatly benefit the customer. Faxon has been computerized since 1958, EBSCO since 1967, Baker & Taylor's Continuations Service since the late 1960s. EBSCO's EBSCONET was the first online system for serials transactions. Faxon followed with the LINX online system.

   Automation in this segment of the serials industry has provided libraries with the opportunity to receive custom management reports on serial holdings, online serials ordering, routing, and even electronic mail.

4. *Marketing is positioning.*

   The Wilson Company has positioned itself as a leading publisher of periodical indexes. The company's image is characterized by quality, thoroughness, and dependability. These attributes can be used to the company's benefit as Wilson enters the online market with its WILSONLINE system. More important, they lend credibility to the authority files, which are depended on for consistency in the print version and which will drive part of the online search system.

5. *Marketing is analysis, planning, and control.*

   The two most important tools of the modern marketer are product analysis and market analysis. They will determine what a firm produces or publishes and who will purchase it.

Product Analysis

Product analysis can be firm- or industry-specific. A company looks at the information or service needs of its customers that could be satisfied by either (a) a new product or (b) changing an existing product. The special library segment of the Wilson Company's customer base is presently the primary user of online searching. By automating its indexes, Wilson can change the format of existing products to meet customer needs.

Other serial publishers became database producers as a byproduct of automation, implementing cost-cutting measures involved in photo-typesetting the printed versions of serial publications. Consequently serial publishers were able to differentiate their products via online databases while holding down the costs of the printed issues.

Market Analysis

My outline of the external market factors that influence a firm in managing its business comes from Frank Daly, manager of market development for Baker & Taylor, whose remarks were published in the 1983 *Book Industry Trends*. The market analysis factors to consider are:

1. Determine who and where is the market.
2. Look at the economic environment: (a) inflation rate, (b) unemployment, (c) interest rates (the cost of borrowing money), and (d) general consumer confidence.
3. Look at the effect of demographics on the marketplace. For the library market: (a) number of students, number of schools, number of libraries; (b) number of professionals in a specific occupation; and (c) professional shifts.

   One can observe the increasing number of online searchers or information managers versus the decreasing number of catalogers as an example of professional shifts. It will have an effect on serial publications marketed to libraries and the format they take.
4. Look at funding levels: (a) federal, ECIA, HEA, LSCA, the size of the appropriations and what can be purchased; (b) state (primarily income) taxes; (c) local (usually property) taxes.

The Library Market

Comments noted here regarding the library market are based on data pulled from the *1983-84 Wilson Marketing Plan*, coauthored by Ruth Miller, market analyst for Wilson. Wilson divides the library market into four segments: (a) school, (b) public, (c) academic, and (d) special—including government—libraries.

The *school library market* is characterized by declining enrollment, which began in 1972 and continues today. Current government statistics (from the National Center for Educational Statistics) do not predict a reversal in the decline until the late 1980s. Acquisitions trends have already been mentioned; they are a decline in book purchases with a concurrent increase in periodical purchases.

The *public library market* is changing. With local tax revenues as the primary funding source, public library performance closely follows that of the national and state economy. *Book Industry* figures show book and periodical expenditures increased and then decreased slightly over the 1980-82 period. The movement can be viewed as a recessionary reaction.

The *academic library market* was characterized by a slight increase in the number of libraries in the 1980-82 period. *Book Industry* figures show little movement in book purchases. Total book and periodical units followed economic movements for the period, increasing and decreasing slightly, while expenditure levels increased substantially over the three-year period, indicating a rising unit cost.

Special libraries comprise many different types of specialized and corporate libraries. BISG (Book Industry Study Group, Inc.) figures indicate special library book acquisitions increased for the 1981-82 and 1982-83 periods, with dollar expenditures increasing as well, due to two factors —increases in the number of units purchased and the rising unit-cost of books.

Periodical purchases for this market are declining. One may assume that with the proliferation of online databases and the availability of document delivery services, special libraries do not need to maintain periodical collections as extensive as before.

Other Market Trends

1. *Serials Industry Systems Advisory Committee (SISAC).*
   Members of the serials industry—publishers, subscription agents, librarians, retailers, and national and international bibliographic database providers—recently formed an industry group to develop standards for computer-to-computer formats for serials. SISAC was conceived under the auspices of the Book Industry Systems Advisory Committee (BISAC) of the Book Industry Study Group, Inc.
2. *Perishability of scientific and business information.*
   Over the past five to ten years, the need for current information has given rise to an increasing number of journals and online databases. There has also been a slight decrease in the total number

of books published. This seems to be true in the pure and applied sciences, though sales have not been quantified as of this writing.

3. *Computerized services of subscription agents and wholesalers.*
These automation features can be viewed as benefit-selling to the librarian. Computerization allows the vendor to produce management reports with greater flexibility and cost efficiency.

4. *Increase in the number of online databases available.*
The increasing number of bibliographic and numeric databases can be viewed, in the free-market economy, as a sign of producers and vendors offering an array of products, in various formats, to compete with each other to meet customers' changing information needs.

As an example of my concept of trends I will suggest the position of H. W. Wilson Company in the marketing-development process. I see Wilson currently between stages three, four, and five.

Stage three is innovation. The Wilson Company has spent the past four years, and millions of dollars, in purchasing hardware and developing software to automate the indexes and develop an online retrieval system—WILSONLINE.

Stage four is positioning. As Wilson enters an established online market, it will draw on its present position in the library community to compete with the entrenched database vendors for a share of this market.

Finally, the last stage is analysis coupled with planning and control. Through demonstrations of the WILSONLINE retrieval system, pilot installations, market questionnaires, and interviews, Wilson is directly soliciting customer input as it designs WILSONLINE and formulates marketing plans to make the system commercially available to the library community. Wilson is taking these steps because the company is shifting its attention to marketing and, as stated in the beginning of this paper: The customer is the key, and focusing on the customer is the objective of marketing.

References

1. Philip Kotler, *Marketing Management: Analysis, Planning, and Control*, 4th ed. (Englewood Cliffs, NJ, 1980), Kotler quoting Drucker, p. 3.

2. Ibid., p. 4.

3. Ibid., pp. 8-9.

4. Book Industry Study Group, Inc., *Book Industry Trends 1983* (New York: Book Industry Study Group, Inc.), table 4, pp. 108-10.

5. Jennifer Cargill, "Vendor Services Supermarket: The New Consumerism," *Wilson Library Bulletin* 57 (January 1983): 395.

6. Kotler, *Marketing Management*, pp. 12-13.

SERIALS STANDARDS (AND GUIDELINES): WHO CARES?

By *Charlotta C. Hensley*

The number of official international and national standards has increased markedly in the past twenty-five years. In 1960, there were 200 International Organization for Standardization (ISO) standards; in 1970, 1600; in 1974, 2500; in 1979, 3750; and in 1983 there were 4917. There were four thousand American National Standards Institute (ANSI) standards in 1974; in 1983 there were more than eleven thousand.

The development of approved standards for library and information science has kept pace, although on a smaller scale. ANSI Committee Z39: Library and Information Services and Related Publishing Practices (ANSC Z39) produced only two standards between 1939 and 1960.[1] In 1965 there were three ANSC Z39 standards; in 1970, six; in 1975, twenty-two; in 1980, thirty-three; and in 1983 there were forty, with nineteen new standards drafted.

Explanations most often offered for this proliferation of standards include the progress of the library profession, which has led to a growing number of accepted practices; the "information explosion," which has created a demand for higher-level services; and the application of computer technology in libraries and publishing.

Serials librarians have long been attentive to standardizing serials formats and bibliographic records. The first ANSC Z39 standard was Z39.1 (1943): *Reference Data and Arrangement of Periodicals*.[2] The first issue of *Serial Slants* contained a lengthy paper calling for standard collations, sizes, and spine lettering of serials bindings, as well as the following resolution:

Be it resolved that:
The A.L.A. Serials Round Table further promote the adoption of uniform

methods of recording reference data for periodicals published anywhere in the nation by any individual, group, society, agency, or commercial publisher.

That these periodicals be checked with American Standards Association, American Standard Reference Data and Arrangement of Periodicals, approved June 7, 1943 (Z39.1-1943) to determine the degree of deviation from standards.

That this work be done by students in Library Schools located in cities where there are sufficiently large collections of serials in special subject fields, since the approach should be by subject.

It is further suggested that the Round Table establish a committee whose duty will be to set up the subject fields in which examination of periodicals will be made; determine which library schools are best located to complete this work and enlist their aid; decide upon subject lists of periodicals to be used as a starting point; and prepare a form to be used by the cooperating schools.

It is also suggested that a local chairman affiliated with the Serials Round Table be appointed in each center where such work is in progress. This person should be responsible for utilizing the information furnished by students to present compelling reasons for requesting uniformity and adhering to suggestions made in A.S.A. Z39.1 to editors.[3]

[Passed at the Serials Round Table meeting, Southeastern Regional A.L.A., Miami, Florida, October 27, 1949]

In 1965 two of the three official ANSC Z39 standards dealt with periodicals.[4] Today there are six ANSC standards devoted specifically to serials, and at least sixteen others (including those dealing with identification codes, information interchange, price indexes, order forms, romanization, and standard addresses) are directly applicable to serials management in libraries.

Serials librarians' current interest in the development and promulgation of standards results primarily from the publication of the second edition of the *Anglo-American Cataloguing Rules* (AACR2) in 1978, as well as from revived interest in the automation of serials records and activities. Endeavors to create machine-readable serials data bases ("one of the most intractable problems in library automation"[5]) have been advanced by the CONSER (Conversion of Serials) project, the national revision of filing rules, and the development of international standards for the bibliographic identification of serials.

Serials Standards (and Guidelines)

The purpose of this paper is to review who develops standards (and guidelines) for serials, what standards are, and what serials librarians think about them. The focus is on the standards that carry either official or *de facto* status within the national library community, rather than those devised for regional or local use.

Definitions and Types

A standard is generally intended to be a level of attainment. The American Library Association (ALA) describes a standard for libraries as "a rule or model of quantity, quality, extent, level or correctness . . . intended as a criterion by which current judgments of value, quality, fitness and correctness are conformed."[6] Types of standards defined by the ALA are the following:

1. *Service or performance standards.* Service standards define a level of excellence or adequacy in performance of library service, typically for a certain type of library or library user. . . .
2. *Technical standards.* Technical standards in library work are similar to industrial standards, and typically provide a measure of excellence or adequacy for a product or thing. . . .
3. *Procedural standards.* Procedural standards describe an acceptable or agreed-upon method of accomplishing a particular type of library activity or task. . . .
4. *Educational standards.* These standards describe requirements for acceptable library education programs. . . .[7]

A guideline is usually a statement of policy that does not carry the force of an official standard. The ALA defines a guideline as "a suggested level of performance or adequacy. . . ."[8]

Development

Standards (and guidelines) pertaining to serials formats and bibliographic records originate in several international and national sources, including official standards organizations, such as the ISO and ANSI; professional associations, such as the International Federation of Library Associations and Institutions (IFLA) and the ALA; government agencies, such as the UNESCO and the Library of Congress (LC); and other authoritative groups, such as the Joint Steering Committee for Revision of AACR (JSCAACR).

International

ISO. The International Organization for Standardization is a voluntary, nonprofit agency comprising eighty-nine member organizations. It oversees the development of official international standards in all fields except electronic and electrical engineering. Of interest to librarians is the work of its Technical Committees (TCs): #6—Paper, Board, and Pulp; #37—Terminology, #42—Photography, #46—Documentation, #97—Information Processing Systems, and #171—Micrographics. Of continual importance is TC 46: Documentation, which is responsible for standards in the areas of documentation, information handling, and librarianship, including related information-interchange systems and networks. Its activities influence abstracting, archival, documentation, and information centers, indexing, information science, libraries, and publishing. In 1983, there were twenty-six participating and twenty-three observer members. Of its thirty published standards, nine are specifically related to serials.

IFLA. The International Federation of Library Associations and Institutions is a nongovernmental, nonprofit organization devoted to international librarianship. It consists of general offices as well as divisions. The development of standards (and guidelines) is an association program carried out by its offices and divisions, often in collaboration. IFLA members have developed guidelines for union catalogs of serials, UNIMARC, and the International Standard Bibliographic Description for Serials (ISBD-S).

UNESCO. UNESCO promotes and disseminates standards for information handling by supporting other organizations and providing services pertaining to archives, documentation, libraries, and scientific and technical information handling at international, regional, and national levels. Of primary interest here is the International Programme for Cooperation in the Field of Scientific and Technical Communication (UNISIST): International Serials Data System (ISDS).

The ISDS was established in 1971 as a worldwide, computerized register, using standardized formats, for the authoritative identification and bibliographic control of scientific and technical serials. ISDS is a dual-level, cooperative network of operational centers.

The International Center in Paris designs and coordinates the system;

creates and maintains the entire data base; assigns International Standard Serial Numbers (ISSNs) and the ISO-designated central authority; and implements international ISSN use. Forty-six regional and national centers designate key-titles, assign or request ISSNs, and promote ISSN use. The ISDS data base is internationally available and now covers all areas of knowledge.

JSCAAR. The Joint Steering Committee for the Revision of the Anglo-American Cataloguing Rules is an international committee of representatives from ALA, LC, the Library Association, the British Library, the Canadian Library Association, and the Library of Australia, and the editors of the second edition of the *Anglo-American Cataloguing Rules* (AACR2). AACR2 is the *de facto* code for serials cataloging practice in the United States.

National

ANSI. The American National Standards Institute is a nonprofit, voluntary federation of more than two hundred labor, professional, technical, and trade standards-writing organizations and nine hundred profit and nonprofit companies. It oversees the voluntary standards system in the United States. It coordinates the development of national standards, provides official United States participation in the activities of nongovernmental international standards organizations, and serves as the clearinghouse and information center for official national standards and international standards.

The committees of ANSI (ANSCs) most directly affecting information services, librarians, and publishers are—Z85: Standardization of Library Supplies and Equipment; Z39: Library and Information Sciences and Related Publishing Practices; X12: Business Data Interchange; X3: Information Processing Systems; PH7: Photographic Audiovisual Systems; and PH5: Micrographic Reproduction.

ANSC Z39 is of most immediate interest to serials librarians. Its purposes are to develop voluntary technical standards pertaining to information products, services, and systems of interest to librarians and publishers, and to encourage the use of its standards in data processing, document delivery, information dissemination and processing, library, and publishing services and systems. In 1983, there were forty-five voting members and seventy-four information members representing federal and library agencies; educational, library, professional, and technical associations; commercial and industrial organizations; publishers; and abstracting and indexing services.

ALA. The American Library Association (ALA), the largest organization representing all areas of librarianship in the United States, develops a variety of widely acknowledged, *de facto* national professional standards and guidelines. In 1982, there were sixty ALA standards and guidelines. Any unit of the ALA may originate a standard for official approval. All divisions have the authority to develop and adopt technical standards for the association; only type-of-library divisions may officially approve nontechnical standards.

Because type-of-activity divisions have had autonomy in developing technical standards for only a few months, activities have heretofore been primarily in representation to ANSI committees and to other standards-developing organizations and in writing guidelines. Of interest to serials librarians are the guidelines developed by the Government Documents Round Table (GODORT) and the Resources and Technical Services Division (RTSD).

LC. The Library of Congress has been a *de facto* standardizing influence on library practices since it began its cataloging distribution service in 1901. Its records are available nationally and internationally on printed cards, in book catalogs, and in machine-readable formats. LC practice is acknowledged in thousands of libraries as authoritative for descriptive cataloging, establishing name and series authority records, assigning subject headings, as well as for formats for machine-readable bibliographic records.

Major bibliographic utilities require conformity to the LC MARC formats and to the *Anglo-American Cataloguing Rules* as interpreted by LC. Serials librarians should be familiar with the CONSER project, the MARC Serials format and distribution service, and the National Serials Data Program (NSDP).

The CONSER (Conversion of Serials) project is a cooperative, international program for creating a machine-readable data base of serials bibliographic records. Begun in 1973, CONSER is managed by the Online Computer Library Center (OCLC). Eighteen CONSER participants standardize serials bibliographic data and add new serials cataloging records, which are then authenticated by LC or the National Library of Canada (NLC) to conform to national and international conventions, rules, or standards for cataloging, as well as for building and maintaining machine-readable bibliographic records.

The authoritative agency for the CONSER program and data base in the United States is LC, as advised by a committee of participants and representatives of professional organizations. There are currently 375,000 CONSER records used by serials librarians for cataloging, union list activities, and creating local machine-readable serials data bases.

The U.S. MARC formats are standards for the representation of machine-readable bibliographic and authority information for various types of library materials. As the most influential communications formats for data structure and element identification in United States libraries, they became the basis for (and are specific implementations of) the more general ANSI Z39.2 (1979) and ISO 2709 (1981) standards for information interchange on magnetic tape. They are maintained by LC staff, who consult with representatives of the ALA, bibliographic utilities, and other agencies.

The MARC Serials format defines serials and describes the record structure, content designation, and record data content to be used in exchanging serials information. An LC/Southeastern Association of Research Libraries Cooperative Serials Project has recently proposed a separate MARC communications format for representing institutional serials holdings information in machine-readable forms. It is intended to be complementary to ANSI Z39.42 (1980) and the proposed ANSI standard for summary and detailed holdings statements. Record layout is similar to other MARC formats, and bibliographic and authority records tags are also consistent.

The National Serials Data Program (NSDP) began operations in January 1968 in recognition that a national serials data base in machine-readable form requires authoritative coordination. The NSDP undertook its ISDS responsibility as the authority for the systematic registration of serials published in the United States in 1973. It currently contributes preliminary, authenticated serials-cataloging information (ISSN, key title, price, address, date of publication) to the OCLC data base for use by the national library community, as well as providing machine-readable records to the ISDS International Center in Paris.

Promulgation

The development and official adoption of standards is the first stage in their use. To have any practical value, standards must be made known to the library community, and then they must be implemented. Although librarians abstractly acknowledge the importance of standardization, the actual degree of practical application is unclear.[9]

Promotion

The United States has a voluntary official standards system. ANSI does not, therefore, actively promote the adoption or use of its standards.

Newly developed standards (and guidelines) are announced to the national library community in professional publications. Their use may be encouraged but cannot be enforced. On the regional or local level, professional attention to standards normally takes the form of meeting programs. The most notable recent example is the LC/ALA Resources and Technical Services Division's regional institutes on AACR2.

Implementation

Planning and sustained effort are required to adjust local practice to conform to internationally or nationally acknowledged standards. The primary interest in doing so is often economic, enforced by the perceived long-range benefit of using a cooperatively developed data base or system in which minimum standards for information types and formats have already been determined.

Literature Review

To make decisions about implementing standards, serials librarians should be aware of them and the reasons they were developed, as well as understanding the implications involved in using them. A principal method of disseminating information about standards is the literature of serials librarianship. The purpose here is to review the journals that serialists acknowledge as primary, specialized information sources in order to determine interest in the promulgation of serials standards.

Method. The years chosen for analysis are 1970 through mid-1983, because this was a period of prodigious development in standards for library and information services, and because four of the five journals identified began after 1970. The serials reviewed are *Library Resources & Technical Services*, the *RTSD Newsletter*, the *Serials Librarian*, *Serials Review*, and *Title Varies*.

Articles identified are devoted to standardization as specifically applicable to serials librarianship. Standards (and guidelines) of interest are those (ISO, ANSI, IFLA, ALA, JSCAACR, UNESCO, LC) developed principally for serials and acknowledged by the national library community. Writing about serials data bases, such as CONSER or union list projects, is also included when discussion of applicable international or national official or *de facto* standards appears. Excluded are announcements, letters, annual and meeting reports, and reviews.

Result. The outcome of this review is shown in table A.

Of the eighty-four articles published in the five journals within the 13½-year period, the largest number (thirty-six) dealt with the revision of the first edition of the *Anglo-American Cataloguing Rules* (AACR) and with the subsequent second edition (AACR2). Secondary areas of interest are general discussions of serials standards development and promulgation[10] (fifteen) and of standardization used in machine-readable serials data bases (fifteen).

The third group (eight) is concerned with official ISO or ANSI standards, primarily the International Standard Serial Number (ISSN) and summary level serials holdings. The remaining articles deal with the diverse topics of the ISBD(S), ISDS, MARC, serials holdings, initialisms, authority systems, and title changes.[11]

Whether this exercise has led to any determination of serials librarians' interest in standards as reflected in their contributions to journal literature is doubtful. It appears, however, that interest in standards promulgation is stimulated primarily by practicability. American librarians, for example, have been directly affected by international catalog code revision because of their use of Library of Congress cataloging, either locally or through cooperative cataloging systems.

AACR2, as interpreted by the Library of Congress, has the force of standardizing cataloging practice in a large number of libraries. Using cooperative machine-readable data bases for serials cataloging and union list projects has also directed interest to standards for the electronic display of bibliographic information. Serials librarians' interest in standards, then, appears to be a practical focus on implementation when forced by circumstances rather than a theoretical discussion of the value of standards to the library community at large.

References

1. Jerrold Orne, "Standards in Library Technology," *Library Trends* 21 (October 1972):287.

2. This standard was first written in 1935.

3. *Serial Slants*, 1 (July 1950):21-22.

4. ANSC Z39.1 (1943/R 1959) and ANSC Z39.5 (1965): *Periodical Title Abbreviations*.

5. Walt Crawford, "Library Automation: Just a Business?" *RTSD Newsletter* 8 (May/June 1983):34.

6. American Library Association Committee on Standards, *Draft ALA Standards Manual* (Chicago: American Library Association, January 1983), pp. 6-7.

7. Ibid., pp. 1-2.

8. Ibid., p. 7.

9. *See* Arnold Hirshon, "International Symposium on the Union Catalog," *RTSD Newsletter* 6 (July/August 1981): 37-40.

10. This category is dominated by the fourteen annual "Year's Work in Serials" reviews in *Library Resources & Technical Services*, all of which include some discussion of serials standards (and guidelines).

11. *Title Varies* is devoted entirely to protesting serials title changes.

Bibliography

1. American Library Association Committee on Standards. Draft *ALA Standards Manual*. Chicago: American Library Association, 1983.

2. Atherton, Pauline. *Handbook for Information Systems and Services*. Paris: UNESCO, 1977.

3. *Catalog of American National Standards*. New York: American National Standards Institute, 1983.

4. Crawford, Walt. "Library Automation: Just a Business?" *RTSD Newsletter* 8 (May/June 1983):32-35.

5. Hensley, Charlotta C. "Serials Automation: A Guide to Applicable Standards." *Serials Review*, in press.

6. ———. "Standards for Resources and Technical Services." (Paper read at the 1982 Spring Meeting of the Colorado Library Association Technical Services and Automation Division, 21 March 1982, at Colorado State University, Fort Collins, Colorado.)

7. Hirshon, Arnold. "International Symposium on the Union Catalog." *RTSD Newsletter* 6 (July/August 1981):37-40.

8. *ISO Catalogue*. Geneva: International Organization for Standardization, 1983.

9. *Library Resources & Technical Services* 14 (Winter 1970)—27 (July/September 1983).

10. Orne, Jerrold. "Standards in Library Technology." *Library Trends* 21 (October 1972):286-97.

11. *RTSD Newsletter* 1 (January 1976)—8 (July/August 1983).

12. Rush, James E., ed. "Technical Standards for Library and Information Science." *Library Trends* 31 (Fall 1982).

13. *Serials Librarian* 1 (Fall 1976)—7 (Summer 1983).

14. *Serials Review* 1 (January/June 1975)—9 (Summer 1983).

15. Szilvassy, Judith. "ISDS: World-wide Serials Control." *IFLA Journal* 8 (1982):371-78.

16. *Title Varies* 1 (December 1973)—6 (December 1980).

17. Vajda, Erik, comp. *UNISIST Guide to Standards for Information Handling*. Paris: UNESCO, 1980.

TABLE A

	LRTS	RTSD Newsletter	Serials Librarian	Serials Review	Title Varies	Total
OFFICIAL						
ISO						
4 (1972)						
8 (1977)						
18 (1981)						
R30 (1956)						
R214 (1976)						
R215 (1961)						
690 (1975)						
*3297 (1975)		1	2	1		4 (5%)
5122 (1979)						
ANSI						
Z39.1 (1977)	1					1 (1%)
Z39.5 (1969/R1974)						
Z39.9 (1979)	(SEE ISO 3297 (1975)					
Z39.39(1979)						
Z39.42(1980)				3		3 (4%)
Z39.45(1983)						
PROFESSIONAL						
IFLA						
ISBD(S)	1				2	3 (4%)
Other						
ALA						
JSCAACR (Revision and AACR2)	10	7	7	4	8	36 (43%)
GOVERNMENT						
Unesco						
ISBD			1			1 (1%)
Library of Congress						
MARC-S						
[MARC holdings]		1	1			2 (2%)
OTHER						
General	14		1			15 (18%)
	(Year's Work)					
Holdings (general)		1				1 (1%)
Initialisms	1					1 (1%)
Serials Data Bases						[15 (18%)]
1. Canada			1			1 (1%)
2. CONSER	1		1	2	1	5 (6%)
3. Union Lists			4	5		9 (11%)
Series Authority	1					1 (1%)
Title Changes		1			[1973-1980]	1 (1%)
	29	10	19	15	11	84 (100%)

APPENDIX I
INTERNATIONAL SERIALS STANDARDS (AND GUIDELINES)

International Organization for Standardization
ISO 4 (1972): *Documentation—International Code for the Abbreviation of Titles of Periodicals*
ISO 8 (1977): *Documentation—Presentation of Periodicals*
ISO 18 (1981): *Documentation—Contents List of Periodicals*
ISO R 30 (1956): *Bibliographic Strip*
ISO R 214 (1976): *Documentation—Abstracts for Publication and Documentation*
ISO R 215 (1961): *Presentation of Contributions to Periodicals*
ISO 690 (1975): *Documentation—Bibliographic References, Essential and Supplementary Elements*
ISO 3297 (1975): *Documentation—International Standard Serial Numbering (ISSN)*
ISO 5122 (1979): *Documentation—Abstract Sheets in Serial Publications*

International Federation of Library and Information Associations
ISBD(S): *International Standard Bibiliographic Description for Serials* (1977)
UNIMARC: Universal MARC Format 2d ed. rev. (1980)

UNESCO
Guidelines for ISDS (1977)
International List of Periodical Title Word Abbreviations (1983)
Joint Steering Committee for the Revision of the Anglo-American Cataloguing Rules
Anglo-American Cataloguing Rules. 2d ed. Chicago: American Library Association, 1978

APPENDIX II

NATIONAL SERIALS STANDARDS (AND GUIDELINES)

American National Standards Institute
Z39.1 (1977): *Periodicals: Format and Arrangement*
Z39.5 (1969/R 1974): *Abbreviation of Titles of Periodicals*
Z39.9 (1979): *International Standard Serial Numbering*
Z39.39 (1979): *Compiling Newspaper and Periodical Publishing Statistics*
Z39.42 (1980): *Serial Holdings Statements at the Summary Level*
Z39.45 (1983): *Claims for Missing Issues of Serials*

American Library Association
Government Documents Round Table (GODORT). *Guidelines for Inputting State Documents into Data Bases* (1982)
Resources and Technical Services Division (RTSD). *Guidelines for Book Catalogs* (1977)

Resources and Technical Services Division. *Guidelines for Handling Library Orders for Serials and Periodicals* (1974)

Resources and Technical Services Division (RTSD). *Guidelines for Union Catalogues of Serials* (1982)

Library of Congress

MARC Serials Editing Guide, 2d. ed. (1978)

National Level Bibliographic Record—Serials (1982)

Serials: A MARC Format, 2d ed. (1974)

Woods, Elaine, ed. *Proposed MARC Format for Holdings and Locations* (December 1, 1982)

TOWARD THE STANDARDIZATION OF BIBLIOGRAPHIC RECORDS IN A PROPOSED STATEWIDE LIBRARY NETWORK

By Carolyn Mueller

In the preface to *The Structure and Governance of Library Networks, Proceedings of the 1978 Conference*, "standardization" appears in a list of unresolved problems demanding immediate attention.[1] Five years later, the issue of standardization is still very much under discussion in numerous articles on communication formats, authority control systems, and the development of standards. Comparatively little information is available on the details of the implementation of bibliographic standards within networks. This paper describes a first step in the latter direction.

Why are bibliographic standards needed? Although there is general agreement on the necessity for technical standards to ensure hardware compatibility, there often is (or seems to be) a tacit assumption that once this compatibility is achieved, information necessarily will be accessible. Unfortunately, physical access to a data base does not necessarily ensure that a known item, or a monograph or serial on a known subject, will be found, even assuming it is present in the data base.

In Williams and Lannom's study of the journal title element in machine-readable data bases, eleven journals were searched in eight DIALOG files. Of 189 forms of the titles of the 11 journals, "[m]ore than 80% varied simply by virtue of differing abbreviations, punctuation, and spacing."[2] Williams and Lannom concluded that

.

> [t]he problem of data element representation is more extensive than most perceive. The number of standards (internal, national, and international) is large, but the use of standards within databases is not widespread.... The result of nonstandardization becomes apparent

when one attempts an exhaustive search on a particular element in multiple databases.[3]

Problems: Initialisms, Acronyms, Etc.

Although Williams and Lannom did not examine the bibliographic data bases of libraries, many of the problems they encountered are likely to be present there as well. Even within a single catalog, punctuation and spacing of the same initialism or acronym may vary if authority control is not strictly maintained. And even assuming uniformity within a single library's bibliographic data base, complete uniformity is most unlikely in a multilibrary network. One network member may use pre-AACR2 headings, or use them only in some instances (perhaps in conversion), and another may use AACR2 headings exclusively. If the network to which the libraries belong does not provide authority control, either library may be unable completely to access the other's holdings.

Similarly, if one has an in-house system that is non-MARC and uses truncated entries; if one does not use uniform titles; if one does not catalog, or does not include in the catalog, serials, documents, or scores; if one uses Library of Congress subject headings and another, Sears' or Hennepin County's; and if libraries are not familiar with each other's local practices—then they may never realize that failure to find an entry for a given title or on a given subject may not mean it is not in the collection.

If the entry is retrieved, there is still the format of local information to contend with—what is entered and where and how. To give but one frequently cited example: Various formats are used to record holdings; some indicate incomplete and missing volumes, and some do not. Consequently, even a relatively simple holdings statement—for example, "1-3,7"—could indicate that volumes one through three and seven are complete and volumes four, five, and six are lacking; that some or all of volumes one through three and seven are incomplete and volumes four, five, and six are lacking; that volumes one through three and seven are complete and volumes four, five, and six are either incomplete or lacking.

One imagines an enormous loose-leaf binder labelled "Local Practices of Network Members." It would list, member by member, all the local idiosyncracies to which libraries are so partial for reasons of cost, clientele, staffing, or history.

These problems and others, which may be present in the most homogeneous of networks, are magnified if the network is heterogeneous, that is, if it includes large and small libraries; special, public, and academic libraries; OCLC, RLIN, and WLN libraries; and libraries using in-house, non-MARC systems, to name but some of the possibilities. Thus, "[w]hile machine-readable files offer the most opportunities to share records and reduce cataloguing costs, sharing can only be successful if *bibliographic* standards are agreed upon and scrupulously followed."[4]

In what follows, by "bibliographic standards" is meant the range of true standards for cataloging and for coding that cataloging into machine-readable form. It also encompasses what might be called *de facto* standards, such as AACR2 and Library of Congress rule interpretations, both of which have attained the status of standards by virtue of their wide application.

The Colorado Experience

Colorado has a number of local networks composed variously of public, academic, and special libraries using a variety of data bases, including OCLC, RLIN, CLSI, DataPhase, and in-house, and a variety of hardware, including Sperry Univac, Tandem, and IBM. A statewide library network is envisioned, and the Network Development Committee, whose members are drawn from each network and the Colorado State Library, has been concerned primarily with the technical standards for machine interfaces.

Interest in the statewide application of bibliographic standards emerged from the Colorado Library Association's Technical Services and Automation Division. Following a nominating committee meeting in summer 1981, three librarians—one from a public library, one from an academic library in another network, and a third from a processing center with no network affiliation—found themselves discussing automation efforts in their libraries.

As they talked, they realized that, while none of the differences in their respective bibliographic data bases presented insurmountable problems to information access, knowing the extent and limitations of each data base would greatly increase the chances of correctly determining the presence or absence of a given monograph, serial, filmstrip, or other item. Standardization would also guarantee the ability to find and interpret the records of a variety of libraries. If decisions on the use of local information fields, for example, were documented and readily available, those who were just beginning to automate (or just beginning to think about automating) would be able to consider the practices of others. As a result, it would be possible to make a compatible choice.

In fall 1981, during the annual convention of the Colorado Library Association, members of the Technical Services and Automation Division met and voted to establish a Bibliographic Standards Committee to identify the bibliographic practices of libraries with machine-readable records. From a list of volunteers, the chair of the division chose five; a sixth, from the Bibliographical Center for Research (BCR), completed the committee's membership.

After the first meeting, the chair of the committee sent a letter to the Network Development Committee to determine whether or not it was planning a similar endeavor and to offer assistance. In the absence of objections, committee members began to develop a questionnaire to be distributed statewide to all types of libraries with machine-readable records. Potential respondents were identified by directors of the state library systems and from a list obtained from BCR of OCLC libraries.

Record Format: Vocabularies

It became apparent very early that many assumptions about record format were invalid and that vocabularies differed; "member record" meant little or nothing to those not using OCLC or RLIN, and MARC tag numbers could prove meaningless to non-MARC respondents, for example. Questions had to be formulated to be understandable to respondents using OCLC MARC, RLIN MARC, and non-MARC formats; to those doing original cataloging; and to those receiving cataloging from a processing center.

A draft questionnaire was discussed during the division's spring meeting in 1982, suggestions were incorporated, and the revised draft was sent to a sample of selected librarians in libraries of different types and sizes. One response indicated that at least one librarian interpreted "standards" to mean 200 percent MARC format, level three AACR2 cataloging for all types of material, and assumed the committee planned to enforce them.

Whether for good or ill, members decided to change the committee's name to the less euphonious Committee to Survey Bibliographic Practices, and rewrote the cover letter. Minor revisions were made to the questionnaire itself, which was subsequently sent to the heads of technical services in eighty-seven libraries in Colorado.

The intent of the questionnaire was to obtain as much information as possible. It included general questions: name of institution, contact person, phone number, type and size of library, presence of machine-readable records and the form in which they are available, membership in a bibliographic utility (to be specified), and plans for further automation. If the respondent had no machine-readable records and was not a member of a utility, s/he was requested to return the questionnaire without completing the remainder.

The general section was followed by questions to determine systems used (acquisitions, cataloging, circulation, online public access catalog, serials check-in), vendor of the system(s), and whether any were integrated. The primary machine-readable bibliographic data base (if more than one was reported) was to be specified, with all questions answered as they applied to that data base. Number of records in MARC and non-MARC formats was to be provided, divided into categories: books, serials, maps, sound recordings, audiovisual materials, manuscripts, and other (to be specified).

Questions about the tagging of records, subject heading lists used, classification systems, use and level of AACR2, updating of records (why and how frequently); about authority control for names (personal, corporate, conference, and geographic), subjects, series, and uniform titles; and about the resolution of conflicts were included. A MARC format-specific list of local information fields was provided, with a request for a description of the information entered in each. The questionnaire was twelve pages long.

Of the eighty-seven libraries to which questionnaires were sent, forty-three responded. One library returned two questionnaires, one for monographs and one for serials. Of the respondents, thirteen indicated they had no machine-readable data base.

Over half of those that did not respond were identified as small special libraries, many of them OCLC users working in consortia. In general, nonrespondents appeared to be OCLC libraries not using, or not subscribing to, OCLC tapes.

Of the thirty-one respondents with machine-readable records, thirteen were public libraries, fourteen were academic libraries, and four were special libraries. Ten were designated small (defined, for the purpose of the survey, as holding up to 100,000 volumes); fourteen, medium-sized (between 100,000 and 500,000 volumes); and seven, large (over 500,000 volumes). Fifteen specified OCLC as their primary data base; four, a data base using another MARC format; six, a combination of MARC and non-MARC formatted records; and six, non-MARC formatted records only.

Survey Report on Practice

When entering new bibliographic records into a data base, all respondent libraries enter personal author (if applicable) and title, and libraries with MARC records consistently supply most other bibliographic data. The greatest variations among libraries using MARC formats are in the tagging of local information.

In general, when adapting Library of Congress, member, or vendor records, if a library accepts one item without verification, it accepts most other items without verification. Libraries are more likely to verify and change information when adapting non-Library of Congress records than when adapting Library of Congress records.

Most of the academic libraries and approximately two-thirds of the public and special libraries use AACR2 for original input of access points for personal, corporate, conference, and geographic names. When adapting machine-readable records, approximately half the respondents always upgrade personal, corporate, conference, and geographic names to AACR2.

Nonserial uniform titles and series in Library of Congress, member, or vendor records are upgraded to AACR2 by fewer than half the libraries, with academic and OCLC libraries upgrading them more often than others. In original input, just over half the libraries provide nonserial uniform titles and series in accordance with AACR2. Many respondents do not include either series or nonserial uniform titles in their bibliographic data bases.

As might be expected, there is heavy reliance on Library of Congress sources (the online authority file, fiche authority file, bibliographic records) for AACR2 headings. Local authority files, both AACR2 and non-AACR2, are the next most heavily used sources, suggesting in the latter case a reluctance to create AACR2 headings not verifiable in an LC source. The fact that non-AACR2 local authority files are preferred to, or at best considered equivalent with, member AACR2 records bears out the frequently stated contention that member-assigned AACR2 headings have a low acceptance rate.

In summary, existing data bases contain both AACR2 and pre-AACR2 records and reflect a diversity of practices, including the use of several different classification schemes and subject heading lists, and variations in the level of AACR2 employed, in the exclusion or inclusion of specific access points and other bibliographic data, and in updating records to reflect changes. Among those using MARC formats, the greatest variations are in the entering and tagging of local information.

Although specific recommendations will not be made at this time, the information gathered (even from so small a sample of libraries) does identify many areas now lacking standardization. A summary report, more complete than that given here, will be published in *Colorado Libraries* and sent to the library systems' directors and the Colorado State Library. The tenure of the former Network Development Committee members has expired; when a new committee has been constituted, a copy of the report will be provided for its use. The complete report, including the questionnaire, will be submitted to ERIC.

Impetus Toward Bibliographic Standards

To generalize from the foregoing, assuming the existence of either the network itself or an individual or group charged with its creation, the impetus to include bibliographic standards may come from within the governing structure or from the outside. If the latter, the governing structure must be identified and the person or group responsible, contacted. It may be necessary to convince him/her/them of the importance of bibliographic standards to the network in order to gain the acceptance or legitimacy implicit in working within the governing structure, in which case the process described here might well provide both convincing data and the information on which to base recommendations.

In either situation, a person or group must volunteer or be appointed or elected to undertake the work that will ultimately lead to standards recommendations to be followed by network members. Although an individual might conceivably be selected, in a less than homogeneous network one person is unlikely to have had enough experience with the variety of practices employed to be able to ask informed questions that will be understood by all respondents.

It is imperative that a diversity of experience be secured to prevent, to the greatest degree possible, such mistakes as assuming that all respondents use a MARC or MARC-compatible format, that OCLC and RLIN MARC are identical in all respects, that all respondents include holdings in their records, and that records are entered and tagged uniformly. In addition, broadly based committee membership can do much to counteract or forestall the ambivalent or negative responses that the issue of standards may evoke if some groups believe they or their interests are not represented.

Determination of Necessary Standardization

Once the individual or group has been selected, areas to be examined for possible standardization should be identified. (Alternatively, this might be the first step, and the group or individual could be selected after this determination is made.) Local information might be selected, or authority control, or bibliographic practices as a whole. Then the present practices of network members and potential members should be identified.

If the network includes (or is to include) existing networks, information about standards and guidelines in use, if any, should be requested; if network software is to be provided by a vendor, copies of user manuals should be obtained, if possible. Information may be gathered by interview (especially if the number of respondents is small in relation to the size of the group collecting the information), or by questionnaire, or a combination of the two.

The usual *caveats* of questionnaire design apply. The information needed must be isolated and defined, and terminology and phraseology must be clear to all respondents. Consideration should be given to how the data will be analyzed so that unanalyzable or unnecessary data are not collected.

The questionnaire should be tested on a representative sample of respondents and any problems identified and resolved before general distribution. The cover letter should explain the reason for the collection of the information, why it is advantageous to respond, and how the results will be disseminated. It should also include a deadline for return that allows enough time for completion but not so much that the questionnaire is lost or forgotten. This deadline also should appear on the questionnaire itself, in case the cover letter is separated from it or inadvertently discarded.

If a committee will analyze the responses, each questionnaire might be divided into sections and the sections distributed among the members. If each committee member is responsible for several related questions, comparisons could be made and summarized readily. (Completed sections should be sent to other members well in advance of the meetings scheduled for their discussion.) A common format should then be selected and an individual or subgroup designated to compile the sections into a coherent whole that would be revised by the entire committee.

After analysis of the questionnaire, the work of the group or individual might extend to recommending areas for standardization and standards or levels of standards based on the information gathered, taking into account national and international standards, *de facto* standards, local network standards and guidelines, vendor requirements, and recurring local practices. The group must also work to secure acceptance of those standards and recommend procedures for their periodic evaluation.

All these matters go beyond the scope of the present paper. As in the situation described above, the work might culminate in a report on areas of common or differing practice, in the hope that this information would prove useful both in planning for the network and in local decision making.

References

1. *The Structure and Governance of Library Networks, Proceedings of the 1978 Conference in Pittsburgh, Pennsylvania*, (New York: Marcel Dekker, 1979), p. iii.

2. Martha E. Williams and Laurence Lannom, "Lack of Standardization of the Journal Title Element in Databases," *Journal of American Society for Information Science* 32, no. 3 (1981): 231.

3. Ibid., p. 229.

4. Jean Whiffin, *Guidelines for Union Catalogues of Serials*, first draft, (The Hague: International Federation of Library Association and Institutions, 1981), p. 19.

STANDARDS AND BIBLIOGRAPHIC AND SERIALS CONTROL IN A MULTICAMPUS/MULTIBRANCH UNIVERSITY LIBRARY SYSTEM

By Georgene E. Fawcett, Judy Johnson, and Sally C. Tseng

In 1975, an analysis of the circulation departments at the University of Nebraska-Lincoln (UNL), the University of Nebraska at Omaha (UNO), and the University of Nebraska Medical Center (UNMC) revealed that because the libraries' collections had doubled—with a concomitant increase in circulation—in the last ten years, the files had proliferated to the point of unwieldiness. No compensatory increase in staffing could be foreseen. Consequently, plans were developed and approved for an automated, computerized circulation system to be implemented as soon as funds could be found. Those funds came as a windfall in 1977; a rider attached to a bill passed by the state legislature gave excess university utility allocations to the libraries at the end of the fiscal year.

Therefore, through negotiation in 1978, the Library Information Retrieval System, otherwise known as LIRS and the local name for the Automated Library Information System (ALIS) produced and distributed by DataPhase, Inc., became a reality. The system included the three autonomous libraries: UNO, UNMC, and UNL with its main library and eleven branches. The libraries' requirements differed.

From the start it became obvious to staff librarians that standards and guidelines had to be developed, agreed on, and abided by. This was imperative because each campus had unique needs and expectations. In addition the DataPhase System has very specific requirements of its own. Although the ALIS programs were based on the MARC format and accepted OCLC tapes to form the data base, the requirements greatly affected what the libraries were allowed to do.

To handle these problems, the librarians convinced the three administrations that two coordinating, policy-setting groups should be formed, one for cataloging and one for circulation. The first meeting of the LIRS Cataloging Group was in October 1978. The Group consisted of representatives from the three major libraries of the University of Nebraska-Lincoln, the University of Nebraska at Omaha, and the University of Nebraska Medical Center. It began by developing policies for monographs; serials, however, soon became the subject of much of the discussion.

Early Concern for Serials

Serials control was and is a major concern for UNMC, as nearly two-thirds of its collection and approximately two-thirds of its circulation are serials. It was essential that UNMC bibliographic data be converted as quickly as possible to allow the circulation of serials on LIRS. The other campuses did not feel the same urgency.

Only UNMC and UNO had computer-generated serials holdings lists when LIRS was established; neither list, however, was in a national standard format. Nonetheless, the use of these lists for possible LIRS conversion was considered. UNO quickly declared it was not possible to use its monthly updated list for conversion purposes. UNMC, however, had recently completed a biennial updating of selected titles representing the majority of the library's serial holdings. Title selection guidelines and data format were based on the Union Catalog of Medical Periodicals (UCMP) system. Ultimately, the UNMC list was selected as the serials base for future development in LIRS.

To meet ALIS requirements, the list had to be converted to MARC format, which was accomplished by identifying conversion tags. Extra funds were allocated for the reformatting, by a commercial firm, of the UCMP records to brief MARC records. Updating of the UNMC serials data base in LIRS would be through OCLC tapes. UNL and UNO were already cataloging their serials on OCLC; UNMC began doing so in 1979.

The sort group numbers from the UCMP format were retained for each title and assigned to MARC field 035. These numbers had been used in list production for sorting the title entries alphabetically by essential word rather than word by word; the former arrangement reflects the title-shelving arrangement of UNMC serials. Sort group numbers continue to be assigned to new titles since they uniquely identify UNMC titles, and, when used in searching LIRS, a UNMC title is retrieved and displayed more quickly than when the alpha search method is used. These numbers are included as part of the bindery slip information to facilitate the updating of item level records.

Again through additional extra funding, temporary staff under the supervision of the circulation department were hired to list individual issue and volume information on worksheets prepared by the serials librarian and to attach optical character-recognition (OCR) labels to the worksheets and corresponding items. These item level records were gathered for the last five years' issues of currently received titles in the reformatted list.

Recognizing the significance of the International Standard Serial Number (ISSN), all available ISSNs were to be added to the reformatted bibliographic data simultaneously with the item level records and their media/location codes. The worksheets containing search keys, ISSNs, sort group numbers, and item level records were converted by a commercial firm to computer tapes for linkage to the bibliographic records. Linkage was to be through the sort group number in the bibliographic and item level records.

Although the ISSNs and search keys from the one tape were successfully linked, the item level records were not consistently complete. Unfortunately, through human error, transport error, or mislabeling and filing error, the remaining six tapes were lost before linkage was made.

Cataloging Standards and Choice of Entry

The key serials issues the LIRS Cataloging Group addressed were cataloging standards and choice of entry. The serials cataloging policies of the three campuses were examined, and a comparative study of the campuses' records and the OCLC data base records was made. The serials study addressed the following issues:

(a) successive vs. latest entries
(b) fullness of records
(c) choice of main entry
(d) handling and treatment of a "serial"

The problem of variant forms of entries was discussed at some length. The example cited was *JAMA: The Journal of the American Medical Association*. The following were the variant forms of entries used:

UNL entered it as: *JAMA: The Journal of the American Medical Association*.
UNMC entered it as: *Journal of the American Medical Association*.
UNO entered it as: *American Medical Association. Journal*.

UNMC, following National Library of Medicine (NLM) practice, cataloged all serials under successive entry; UNL cataloged all new titles under successive entry; and at UNO the policy varied. UNMC intended to print its serials list updates from the LIRS records, and retaining its choice of entry was necessary for that purpose.

The LIRS Cataloging Group developed the following documents after consulting the *Anglo-American Cataloguing Rules* (AACR1[1] and AACR2[2]), *Guidelines for ISDS*,[3] *CONSER Manual*,[4] *Fixed and Variable Field Tags for Serial Records Used in the OCLC System*,[5] *Level I and K Input Standards*,[6] *MARC Serials Editing Guide, CONSER Edition*,[7] and LC rule interpretations in *Cataloging Service Bulletins*,[8] namely:

(a) Cataloging Standards for All Formats
(b) Guidelines for Serials Entries
(c) Guidelines for Determining Successive Serials Records

It was generally agreed that *AACR2* choice of main entry and the *OCLC Level I Input Standard* would apply to serial bibliographic records.

The group decided that UNO and UNL would catalog under successive entry all titles held in common with UNMC, regardless of beginning date of publication. For records not held in common, the CONSER guidelines would apply. They state that serials titles with a beginning date of 1967 or later are to be cataloged under successive entry. Titles beginning in 1966 or earlier may be cataloged as either successive entry or latest entry.

Name Headings, Master Records

The different forms of name headings established by the Library of Congress (LC) and the National Library of Medicine (NLM) presented another major problem for the local system. No automated authority control was foreseeable at that time. The LC name headings file, which included superimposition, was accepted as the name authority for UNL and UNO. The NLM name headings file was accepted as the authority for UNMC. It was agreed that once AACR2 was implemented, all three campuses would use the same form of name heading.

The group also agreed that the first record entering the system was to be the master record. This decision, however, caused problems. For example, if a partial record were entered first by one library and later another library cataloged the same title with more bibliographic data, the system would not accept the second record; it would reject it as a duplicate. To provide a full bibliographic record, the partial record had to be upgraded, with additional access points and data entered manually by the second library.

One of the goals of LIRS was to list serial titles housed and acquired by the University of Nebraska Libraries in order to facilitate their use among the wider library community. Initially, the records of these titles were intended to satisfy bibliographic needs as well as the requirements of interlibrary loan and other forms of library cooperation. Specific library location and holdings of each campus were also to be included. High-quality and LC-level bibliographic records were emphasized.

The group also looked into the definition of "serial." It was recognized that certain types of continuations—such as almanacs, directories, monographic series, and yearbooks—were often treated differently than periodicals. What might be treated as a serial by one campus was not necessarily treated as such by another. This was especially true with monographic series. One library might choose to treat the series as monographs and catalog each issue separately, whereas another library might treat it as a serial and catalog or classify all the issues together, possibly some with analytics. The group determined that no common treatment would be enforced.

The Holdings Component

A standardized holdings statement based on the *American National Standard Serial Holdings Statement at the Summary Level, Draft #8, 4/20/79* was developed. After consultation with staff at the Library of Congress and the National Library of Medicine, tag 890 was selected for the placement of the holdings statement that appears in the bibliographic record and on the serials screens.

The LIRS Statement was formatted to accommodate the needs of the three campuses. Although each campus required holdings, UNL, with its multiple locations, also required a display of holdings for each location. UNMC provided users with specific search-key requirements and allowed for Serline, NLM's biomedical serials holdings data base, reporting. Restrictions of statement length were imposed by LIRS and NLM's Serline reporting requirements.

Currently, only UNMC is attaching the 890 to its OCLC records, despite the problems that developed:

Multiple 890's appear on a shared bibliographic record but are not repeatable on the serials screen; only the first 890 appears on the serials screen. Even though several libraries hold a particular title, only one library is identified on the serials screen as the holding library, that being the library which entered the first 890 field.

The holdings display is not user-friendly.

UNMC incomplete holdings are not shown because of NLM's format restrictions.

Online Circulation to Online Catalog

By now it is probably apparent to the reader that LIRS had become more than an online circulation system—it had become an online catalog. (DataPhase had informed the directors that LIRS could develop into one.) Unfortunately, it was not apparent just how much room the records were using, nor how fast various files on the data base were being filled.

Because of the hardware configuration more disk drives could not be added. The only option was to change to a larger computer (a financial impossibility) or reduce and compact the records. The latter course was chosen. Then the Cataloging Group agonized over what constituted a usable (rather than an excellent) bibliographic record, and it finally completed the dismal task by choosing which tags could be stripped from the records.

The content of bibliographic records for serials had used full MARC-S, including all applicable tags, indicators, and subfields. The index fields were authors, titles, variant titles, series, subjects, LC card numbers, OCLC number, and ISSN. Although the initial stripping decisions were made in 1980, other fields had to be stripped in 1982. Bibliographic records may now include only leader information, OCLC number, fixed field information, LC card number, holding library codes, local identification numbers, main entry, title, edition, imprint, serial numerical/alphabetical/chronological designation, generalized serial holdings statement, local editing code, and local processing information. LIRS once again became a circulatory inventory system.

After making the decisions about which tags to strip, the data base was off-loaded to run against the stripping program. Then it was re-loaded, and LIRS began functioning again as an online circulation system only. As each new OCLC archival tape is received, it is duplicated, and the original archival tape is stored for any possible future uses. The duplicate is stripped of the unwanted tags and loaded on the data base.

In the future, if money for a larger computer becomes available, the process can be reversed.

ALIS I to ALIS II

Unfortunately, what was unknown at the time, and what DataPhase had neglected to disclose, was that each record has a leader that includes lengthy machine-readable information that must be attached to each record. This information and the fixed field information are mandated by the standards and cannot be controlled by the agency. None of it could be stripped. Consequently, not nearly as much space was saved as had been envisioned, and two years later the files again had to be rearranged to gain time while options—either to buy larger equipment or to convert from ALIS I to ALIS II software, which uses space much more efficiently—were studied.

The libraries opted for the latter and are serving as the alpha site for conversion. To coordinate the conversion, the cataloging and circulation groups have merged into one—the LIRS Coordinating Committee (LCC). To date, because the summer and fall have been dedicated to conversion, it has met infrequently.

The LCC has requested that ALIS II have the capability for serials screens to be campus-specific in holdings displays. The American National Standards Institute (ANSI) is rewriting the holdings statement standards. The LCC will need to reevaluate and rewrite the LIRS 890 statement to be compatible with the new ANSI statement. UNMC now participates in PHILSOM (Periodical Holdings in Libraries of Schools of Medicine) for serials control. Since PHILSOM is not in MARC format, there is no interface with LIRS. PHILSOM assumes the responsibility for reporting its members' holdings to NLM. Consequently, UNMC may no longer be restricted to NLM's format for creating holdings statements.

While all the various national standards bring uniformity and consistency to the very unruly world of serials, it is going to be quite some time before any vendor can conquer the problems of a multicampus, multilibrary system. The serials inquiry function in ALIS II is at least a year away, and if past experience presages the future, the assumption can safely be made that the serials inquiry function will not be realized in that time.

In the move from ALIS I to ALIS II, serial capabilities have actually decreased. When the system switch is complete, the record that appears on the screen will look like a monographic record until the ALIS II software is enhanced. Also, volumes will be listed by OCR number and not in numerical volume/part sequence. Thus, the software transition made because of space restrictions has not solved all serial problems for the University of Nebraska system. The full benefits of serials in LIRS are yet to be realized.

References

1. *Anglo-American Cataloging Rules. North American Text*. (Chicago: American Library Association, 1967).
2. American Library Association [Michael Gorman and Paul W. Winkler, eds.], *Anglo-American Cataloging Rules*, 2d ed. (Chicago: American Library Association, 1978).
3. International Centre for the Registration of Serial Publications, *UNISIST: International Serials Data System. Guidelines for ISDS* (Paris: UNESCO, 1973).
4. *CONSER Manual* (Washington: Council on Library Resources, 1977).
5. *Fixed and Variable Field Tags for Serial Records Used in the OCLC System*. (Columbus, OH: OCLC, Inc., 1978).
6. *Level I and K Input Standards* (Columbus, OH: OCLC, Inc., 1977).
7. Phillis A. Bruns and Mary E. Sauer, *MARC Serials Editing Guide: CONSER Edition* (Washington: MARC Development Office, Library of Congress, 1975) plus updates.
8. *Cataloging Service Bulletin*, no. 1 (summer 1978)-. (Washington: Cataloging Distribution Service, Library of Congress, 1978-).

LOCALLY DEVELOPED STANDARDS—BENEFICIAL OR ANATHEMA?

By Marjorie E. Adams

At the outset of this volume, Norman Stevens stated that an understanding of standards and their development is common among librarians. Yet how many librarians, before attending a conference on standards, could have named more than one or two standards that affect their day-to-day professional work? How many could have described the process of standards development?

It is not an exaggeration to state that every facet of library and information science is affected by some kind of standard—whether a guideline or model, a technical specification, or a procedural rule.[1] Just as the standards that guide or govern library activities take varying forms (some descriptive, some prescriptive), the process of standards development varies: Certain standards have developed over a long period of time through use (*de facto* standards);[2] others have been deliberately created by a standards-development body. Some standards have received the informal acceptance of users, or the formal approval of a voting group (*de jure*[3] or *ex cathedra*[4] standards); they may have emanated from a standards organization, a governmental body, a professional organization or interest group, or an institution or body of recognized authority. Other standards have developed or have been created internationally, nationally, in a network, or locally.

The topic of this paper is locally developed standards. Questions often raised about locally developed standards include: Why are local standards necessary? How are they developed? Aren't local standards by definition provincial or parochial, inherently narrow in scope and outlook? Isn't the potential for conflict with national standards reason enough to refrain from making local standards? In short, are locally developed standards beneficial or anathema?

Standards Development Group

To frame an answer to those questions I shall describe the recent experience in local standards development at the Ohio State University Libraries (OSUL) by a group currently called the Subcommittee on LCS Holdings Records. I shall describe the elements that need to be considered when examining any standard: What is the purpose and membership of the standards-development group? For whom are the standards intended? What is the process of standards development and implementation? For what reasons, and in what context, are the standards developed? What is the impact of the standards?

Purpose

The purpose, as well as the name,[5] of the Subcommittee on LCS Holdings Records has changed at least three times during its nine-year life span. The committee was first established, in 1974/75, to develop the specifications needed by the programmers who were designing the volume holdings file component of LCS, the Library Control System, OSUL's online public-access catalog/circulation system. The committee next planned and developed rules for the conversion of the data from OSUL's manual union list file to the newly designed automated holdings file. Currently, the committee's purpose is to refine the Holdings File by developing formats and rules for the input of additional data and by defining procedures for uses of the Holdings File in various library operations.

These changes in the committee's functions demonstrate the evolutionary nature of standards—that standards are dynamic and ever-changing, that they build on previous development. The committee has observed that the implementation of initial standards has created a demand for additional standardization, and, in many cases, additional standards can be built on the logic and format of the committee's previous work.

Users

The standards the committee has developed take the form of specifications, rules, and procedures, and are intended to benefit all users of LCS, in both public and technical services operations, at OSUL (and the State Library of Ohio, an independent local LCS user). Although library patrons are the ultimate users of the system, they generally remain unaware of the standards that undergird its processes and procedures. The primary standards user group, then, is the library staff, as they engage in their information access and interpretation functions.[6]

Membership

The committee's membership represents all users of LCS—the OSUL and the State Library; technical and public services; administrator and practitioner; professional and support staff; department libraries and main library; cataloging, acquisitions, reference, and circulation departments. The committee currently has ten members, some members "wearing two hats." Over the years individual membership has rotated, but overall the group has maintained a membership widely representative of the LCS user community.

Process

The committee is energetic and productive, but the production of final documents is painstakingly slow, or at least so it seems to the members of the committee. The pace, typical of standards development, is tempered by the process employed. It is a consultative, essentially political process that in the extreme could proceed as follows: Survey needs; discuss in committee; draft standard; hash and rehash in committee; redraft; consult with users of the system; discuss in committee; compromise; redraft (perhaps even redesign); submit revision to various groups; hold hearings; discuss in committee; revise as necessary; submit to approving body, i.e., the library administration; rework (perhaps); prepare final draft; resubmit to approving body; reproduce; disseminate to users; and *finally* implement.

This scenario illustrates what David Kaser has described as the "great pains [taken by a standards-development group] to seek the advice of . . . groups and individuals and to keep the relevant publics informed at every point in its deliberations." He goes on to say that the "responses [and criticisms help] to sharpen the committee's working drafts, to bring them more fully into accord with . . . consensus, and ultimately, to make [the final product] tolerable to a substantial majority. . . .[7] As the foregoing describes, the development of standards requires an enormous effort on the part of all, if the standards are to be worthy and capable of implementation.

Implementation

As with most standards in the library profession, implementation of LCS Holdings File standards is in large part voluntary. At OSUL, for example, staff in the various libraries can be trained to perform online maintenance, which means they can change certain information in the Holdings File at terminals in their locations. Although supervisors carry the big stick of deauthorization of this remote online maintenance capability, they speak softly, and compliance with the standards depends mostly on gentle persuasion and subtle pressure.

Primarily, though, successful implementation has its roots in the standards-development process itself. If the users of the standard have a broad understanding of the necessity and advantages of adherence to the standard, and if that understanding is fostered by involvement in the creation of the standard, the completed standard likely will already have the consensual acceptance necessary to make implementation a relatively easy follow-up step.

Another factor affecting successful implementation is the necessity for wide and methodical dissemination of the standard, in written form, by way of illustration in news releases, and at workshops. As ANSC Z39 has experienced, this critical step leading to successful application can be difficult, and more effort in this regard could have a positive effect on the situation.[8]

Context

With the huge amount of effort required in local standards development and implementation, it behooves the keepers of the local system to be sure they are not reinventing the wheel or, worse yet, rejecting a nationally standard wheel. Local standards might well be developed in ignorance of an existing national standard, or, in rarer instances, could consciously reject a national standard.

But it is more likely the case that local standards are developed as a result of a need unfulfilled by national or international standards. OSUL found itself in that situation in 1974/75, when developing specifications for the LCS Holdings Files. Serial holdings standards were needed for both summary and detailed levels; yet, with standards development being the slow process it invariably is, ANSI standard Z39.42 for *Serials Holdings Statements at the Summary Level* did not appear until 1980, and the *Standard for Detailed Holdings* is still in draft.

Local standards development predating the creation of a national standard obviously can contribute to the latter by offering a base of experience and introducing principles that later can be incorporated into the national standard. In the case of the *Serial Holdings Statements at the Summary Level*, experience at Chemical Abstracts, among other organizations, contributed in this manner to the final national product.

Reasons for Local Standards

Why in 1974/75 did OSUL, after a century of library service, turn its attention to standards for serial holdings? A familiar ring can be heard in the answer, "The computer made us do it." For both technical and nontechnical reasons computer technology has compelled standardization around the world in all areas of endeavor.

At OSUL the initial impetus for the standardization of serial holdings was the technical need of programmers for precise specifications on which to base the design of the Holdings File. An equally important impetus was the nontechnical desire to provide patrons with quick, reliable, and multiple-point access to consistent information about serials holdings. With the advent of an online Holdings File the hundreds of thousands of serial holdings in some forty library locations were soon to be accessible to anyone at a terminal.

Without standardization, the myriad conventions used over the years in the manual serial file would probably have produced what Frans Heymans would call "nothing but a Babelographic tower"[9]; with standardization, LCS could offer what Heymans terms "human-useable"[10] information. Clearly, standardization provides the following advantages to a system such as LCS:

1. It provides a common format for representing the holdings of all libraries sharing the system. Data elements, hierarchies, and meanings are consistent.
2. The common format provides elements of a common language, which is the basis for communicating and sharing information within the system, between service points as well as with patrons.

3. Consistency fosters accuracy and quality control, ultimately improving service to patrons.
4. The logically principled structure allows computer manipulation of data (e.g., sequencing and searching of holdings) and encourages enhancements of the system.
5. Standardization provides economy and efficiency of operation (e.g., in training of staff).

Impact

Beyond these advantages, the standards development *process* can have a substantially positive impact on the local system. It may be felt in the following ways:

1. Involvement in the process of local standards development can create an environment for the acceptance of national and international standards. Involvement provides first-hand experience with the advantages of standardization and creates the demand for additional standards.
2. Local efforts to develop standards can reinforce the importance of continuous awareness of national and international standards activity and of contributing to that process.
3. Experience gained in local standards making can contribute to an understanding of the larger standards-development process. The local experience fosters tolerance and patience with the pace and the consultative nature of the process, and demonstrates the importance (if implementation is to be successful) of active dissemination of the final standards products.
4. The evolutionary nature of standards themselves will, without a doubt, move the system forward, propelling it toward new service objectives that certainly will require the use of national and international standards. Florence Murray, writing about Canadian library standards, sums it up by stating, "Library standards reflect the objectives and priorities of the [system] that produces them, and change as the [system] changes.... Standards, if successful, have a short active life; they promote the development of service that makes possible new objectives that in turn demand new standards."[11]

It is in examining the advantages of locally developed standards and assessing the impact of the local standards-development process that the answer is found to the question posed in the title of this paper, "Locally Developed Standards—Beneficial or Anathema?" The description of the experience at the Ohio State University Libraries was offered to illustrate that locally developed standards can be intrinsically beneficial, not so much as ends in and of themselves but as the beginning of a dynamic process, or a trip, if you will. It starts with a local view, broadens perspective along the way, contributes to the collective national experience, and leads to a demand for national and international standards.

References

1. Professional Board, "IFLA and ISO Standards Work," *IFLA Journal* (1982):325.

2. Robert W. Frase, "Procedures for Development and Access to Published Standards," *Library Trends* 31 (Fall 1982):225.

3. Ibid.

4. Warwick S. Cathro, "The Upheaval in Bibliographic Exchange Standards 1974-1984," *Australian Library Journal* 29 (May 1980):59-66; also cited in Peter Harvard-Williams, "International Standards," *Library Trends* 31 (Summer 1982):174.

5. This group has also been known as the Task Force on Serial Holdings, the Task Force on Serial Implementation, and the Task Force on the Changeover to On-line Serial Records. For most of its history it has been chaired by Susan Logan, Coordinator of Library Automation, who also chairs the On-line Catalog Committee, of which this group is a subcommittee.

6. Sandra K. Paul and Johnnie E. Givens, "Standards Viewed from the Applications Perspective," *Library Trends* 31 (Fall 1982):331, 340.

7. David Kaser, "Standards for College Libraries," *Library Trends* 31 (Summer 1982):14.

8. Sandra K. Paul and Johnnie E. Givens, "Standards Viewed," p. 332.

9. Frans Heymans, "How Human-Usable Is Interchangeable? Or, Shall We Produce Catalogues or Babelographic Towers?" *Library Resources and Technical Services* 26 (April/June 1982):168.

10. Ibid., pp. 156-69.

11. Florence B. Murray, "Canadian Library Standards," *Library Trends* 21 (October 1972):309.

Bibliography

1. Berger, Patricia Wilson. "Standards." *ALA Yearbook* (1982):285-88.

2. Bloss, Meredith. "Research and Standards for Library Service." *Library Research* 2 (Winter 1980):285-308.

3. Hirsch, Felix E., ed. "Standards for Libraries." *Library Trends* 21 (October 1972).

4. Jones, Arthur. "Standards, Objectives and Guidelines: Their Relevance in Librarianship." *IFLA Journal* 8, no. 3 (1982):278-81.

5. Rush, James E., ed. "Technical Standards for Library and Information Science." *Library Trends* 31 (Fall 1982).

6. Weech, Terry L., ed. "Standards for Library and Information Services." *Library Trends* 31 (Summer 1982).

THE SERIALS INFORMATION CHAIN: WORKING TOGETHER TOWARD A COMMON GOAL

By John B. Merriman

The story begins in the 1960s, the era of a great bonanza in librarianship and publishing. They were heady times indeed. New libraries with insatiable demands for books and journals and new and established publishers quickly took full advantage of the sellers' market for both new materials and retrospective collection building, particularly the demand for reprints.

The information explosion had begun. Status, self-esteem, research, professional standards, and the academic rat race demanded current and comprehensive collections. The serial had come into its own as the primary source of up-to-date information. An ever-increasing percentage of library budgets was allocated for serials acquisitions. Although serials were widely recognized as important sources and disseminators of information, now, at last, their full importance was recognized—or was it?

Unfortunately, in many libraries the handling of serials was regarded as a routine clerical task. One ordered or renewed a year's subscription, paid the publisher's/vendor's bill, checked in and routed the issues as they arrived each day. What was this, when compared with the mystique of book selection, cataloging, and classification? In spite of the pioneering work of A. D. Osborn in 1955 (the year in which he published his classic *Serials Publications: Their Place and Treatment in Libraries*), the serials department in the main was the poor relation in the family.

The same pattern could be discerned in the offices of publishers, where resources were poured into the editorial and production departments. The vital distribution side was treated as a Cinderella, with low-grade, ever-changing staff and inefficient clerical processes that were not conducive to rapid growth. In other cases, publishers put their trust in so-called fulfillment agencies, and sometimes even in the printer. Because distribution was regarded as a routine clerical job, many publishers were sold computer packages that were entirely unsuited to the task, and the results were horrific. Everybody in the information chain suffered.

At the same time there appeared to be little awareness of librarians' needs. Arbitrary decisions were made about changes in format, title, extra volumes, supplements, and TPIs (Title-Page Indexes). All this caused much frustration and gnashing of teeth amongst serials librarians.

After the frenetic sixties, what was the new decade going to bring—a period of consolidation and common sense, or the moment of truth? By the beginning of the 1970s Ulrich listed 50,000 periodicals and 20,000 irregular serials and annuals. It was a decade marked by a number of significant events:

1972   Clara D. Brown's *Serials: Acquisition and Maintenance*. A manual concerned with the down-to-earth organization of a non-automated serials department. In 1980 it was superseded by a new and enlarged edition under the title *Serials: Past, Present and Future*.

1973   First appearance of *Title Varies*, a fun magazine with a serious purpose. A "cri de coeur" addressed to the publishers from frustrated serials librarians.

1974   Faxon's Serials Updating Service began.

1975   First appearance of *Serials Review*.

1975   Publication of Katz and Gellatly's *Guide to Magazine and Serial Agents*.

1976   First appearance of *Serials Librarian*. It is interesting and very significant that the editorial board included those doyens of subscription agents—Frank Clasquin of Faxon and Eleanor Vreeland, Vice President of Stechert-Macmillan. The trade was beginning to be perceived as having something to offer librarians.

So far, the important events I have mentioned all took place in the U.S.A.

United Kingdom Activities

I must now turn to the U.K., where the pattern of growth in libraries and publishing had been very similar to that of the U.S., but naturally on a smaller scale. Blackwell's subscription division had expanded to a size that was inconceivable when I joined the company in 1955.

As an ex-librarian, I became concerned that although they were in the middle of an information explosion, the main participants—authors, publishers, vendors, librarians, and readers—were poles apart. Communication among them was minimal. The library profession, including library schools and the professional press, hardly admitted the existence of serials management as a distinct discipline. Regrettably this view still applies in most British schools of librarianship today.

In 1974 I became more and more concerned about the lack of a forum not only for an exchange of ideas between the trade and librarians but among practicing serials librarians themselves. Blackwell's decided to take the initiative. We wrote to the librarians of all the higher educational institutions (universities and polytechnics) in the U.K. and the Republic of Ireland, inviting them to send a representative to a conference to be held at Christ Church College, Oxford, on 10 and 11 April 1975. The theme was to be "The Acquisition of Periodicals in Academic Libraries."

The aim of the conference was to bring together periodicals librarians from universities and polytechnics to hear the views of representatives from the publishing and subscription agency fields. We also wanted to provide a forum for discussion for those people in academic libraries faced with common problems of the supply and acquisition of periodicals. A small number of journal and microform publishers were also invited. The response was overwhelming. Eighty percent of the invited academic institutions sent representatives.

The United Kingdom Serials Group

And so the embryonic U.K. Serials Group (although at the start it was envisaged as the Serial Librarians Group) was born amidst the mediaeval splendor of Christ Church. It was, however, quickly realized that this title was too restrictive.

From the outset I was determined it should be an independent group, able to stand on its own feet and not be beholden to any other trade or professional organization or commercial company. An ad hoc committee of librarians was set up to study the feasibility of setting up an organization, but unfortunately little was achieved.

In 1976 I was asked if I would organize a second conference in the spring of 1977. This I agreed to do, on the understanding that it must be the last to run under the Blackwell's banner. The conference resulted in the first of the Group's publications: *Serials Monograph No. 1: Economics of Serials Management* (Proceedings of the 2nd Blackwell's Periodicals Conference held at Trinity College, Oxford, March 23-24, 1977).

At the same time a small group of enthusiasts formed another ad hoc committee, again to try to form an independent group. One thing we had to decide was whether or not to come under the umbrella of an already well-established professional body, such as SCONUL (Standing Conference on National and University Libraries), the Library Association, or the Association of Special Libraries and Information Bureaux (ASLIB). For various reasons none of these august bodies really wanted us, mainly because our membership was too wide and consisted of a mixture of trade and library professionals. We decided to make a burst for freedom and independence and have never regretted it.

A great deal of credit must be given to David Woodworth of the School of Librarianship, Loughborough Technical College, who acted as secretary, and David Wood of the British Library, Lending Division, who acted as chairman. At the conference in York in 1978 the Group finally got off the ground. A constitution was adopted, officers and committee were elected, aims and objectives defined.

The primary aims are to bridge the gap between the producer and the end user of serials and to provide a forum for the interchange of information, ideas, suggestions, and the solution of problems. Members represent the common interests of librarians, vendors, publishers, and information workers.

The main objectives of the Group are:

- To encourage and promote a continuing discussion of serials and associated areas among all interested parties in the information industry, both nationally and internationally.
- To develop and maintain links among all concerned with the production, distribution, and use of serials.
- To encourage professional awareness in all who work with serials.
- To encourage and assist the development of appropriate research in the field of serials management.
- To be the natural articulator of serials management in the U.K.

Membership is open to anyone in the information industry. There is a small membership fee of $15, which includes a copy of the conference proceedings and the twice-yearly newsletter. At present all officials work on a voluntary basis.

Activities of the U.K.S.G.

The annual conference is the U.K.S.G.'s most important activity. It begins with the opening of the trade exhibition on a Monday afternoon and disperses after lunch on the following Thursday. The trade exhibition includes publishers, subscription agents, and binders, and is a very popular feature. It has covered a number of themes: Economics of Serials Management, Financing the Serial from Producer to User, Automation and Serials, Resource Sharing—Its Impact on Serials, and The Information Chain. (We are now coming away from the idea of a theme, believing it imposes undesirable constraints. In the future we intend to identify important issues to be included under the all-embracing title "The Annual Serials Conference." The proceedings of the conferences are published as a monograph series, and members receive copies as part of their subscription.

Short courses are organized at regular intervals in major cities of the U.K. Each is limited to two days and the numbers attending to not more than twenty-five. As far as possible we use local experts as course tutors, but we do have a few specialists to call on when needed. These courses cover finance and serials control, periodical administration, serials automation, agents and their services, bibliography of serials, etc. The level of the courses varies. Some are aimed at senior and middle management, others are for junior clerical assistants.

It appears serials librarians are hungry for these courses, which are always oversubscribed. (I think this is a sad reflection on the British library schools, which, with two exceptions, totally neglect serials education.) The courses are well supported by staff from publishers and subscription agencies.

We have an active publishing program, with a twice-yearly newsletter, serials monographs, *Directory of Title Pages, Indexes and Contents Pages (DOTIC)*, and *Current British Journals*. Other publications are planned, including a bibliography of serials librarianship. There is also the possibility of upgrading the newsletter into a journal that would be available to nonmembers by subscription.

One developing feature of the newsletter is the "grumble page," which encourages contributions from members who have problems with serials. The U.K.S.G. then hopes through collective pressure to bring about improvements.

At present we are facing a number of issues vital to the future of the Group. The first is: Should the Group become more international in scope? Until now it has been run by and dedicated to the needs of all who work with serials in the U.K. We have, however, been pleased to welcome members from overseas, and our conferences have been enhanced by their presence and contributions. Indeed our 1984 conference is something of a special event, as we will be welcoming a group from the U.S.A., which will include both speakers and delegates. Nancy Jean Melin, the editor of this volume, is masterminding the organization of this conference. There is, however, a fear amongst some of our members about a loss of identity if we become too large and international.

I believe serials issues transcend national boundaries, although I do not have great faith in large international organizations. I believe the correct route is to build up strong organizations within countries, and then perhaps link them together in some kind of international federation.

Our second area of concern, quite frankly, is managing success. As is almost always the case, we have been driven forward by a small group of unpaid enthusiasts who have shouldered increasingly heavy burdens. We have now just about reached the stage of employing our first paid part-time officer. Everyone knows only too well how easy it is for a bureaucracy to arise, often inhibiting the realization of the aims and ideals of the founders (and greatly increasing overhead costs and, eventually, the sums members pay for their subscriptions).

I have tried in this paper briefly to set the scene historically, to show how the embryo of an idea developed into the present U.K.S.G., to examine its activities, and the way ahead. An organization that brings together librarians, publishers, and vendors can draw on tremendous backup resources, expertise, and knowledge. It can act positively and get on with the job, and that is what it is all about. We sincerely hope similar organizations will be formed outside the U.K.

EDUCATION FOR SERIALS LIBRARIANSHIP: A BRITISH LIBRARY RESEARCH PROJECT

By David P. Woodworth

At the 2nd Library Seminar on Serials, held in Columbus last year, I presented a paper on serials education* and described the syllabus we follow at Loughborough University. The present paper is supplementary in that I intend to outline the results of the British Library-supported research project on which I have been working during the last year. It is on the teaching of serials in U.K. library schools.

The terms education and training are, like coffee and milk, often used together without a second thought given to the difference between them. Education can take the following forms:

1. Full- or part-time. (More or less the sole prerogative of the library schools.)
2. In-house or on-the-job training. (The extent to which it is applied will vary, depending on time, expertise and, frankly, ability or interest.)
3. Continuing education—refresher/follow-up courses.

The growth in the importance of serials requires an overall appreciation of the subject, and only through some form of education will it be achieved. Unfortunately, the appreciation of the advantages of education varies considerably from librarian to librarian and indeed from library school to library school.

---

*"Serials Education: A UK Viewpoint" in *Serials and Microforms: Patron-Oriented Management* (*Proceedings of the Second Annual Serials Conference and Eighth Annual Microforms Conference*), ed. Nancy Jean Melin (Westport, CT: Meckler Publishing, 1983), pp. 117-26.

I have long believed that many senior librarians and educators are Literary Luddites who wish their many professional problems would, quite simply, go away; instead, as the Sorcerer's Apprentice found, they have multiplied.

To try and assess the situation, and because there *appeared* to be inconsistent (if any) coverage of serials in U.K. library schools, this investigation was initiated. It was intended to:

(a) determine the current status of serials education,

(b) find out whether the customer (i.e., the practitioner) was getting what he or she wanted from the professional library institutions, *and*

(c) attempt to make suggestions for future coverage.

Right now all serials education is inferior to that for books and other literature. The high number of students who enter public library service may explain this situation, at least in part. In fact, a quick glance through the *World Guide to Library Schools and Training Courses* reveals coverage as diverse as one would wish to see. It is not my brief to argue the case for or against the fragmentation of syllabi, but it must make some form of standardization of practice difficult to attain.

What of serials? Until 1983 only one school treated serials in any way seriously, with a separate option devoted to the coverage of all aspects and occupying periods of the timetable throughout the academic year. Manchester Polytechnic, however, has now expressed its intention to introduce comprehensive coverage of serials in its postgraduate syllabus and increased coverage in its undergraduate courses.

On the other hand, a course announced by CLW entitled "Degree of Master of Arts in Periodical Studies" is *not* what it appears; it is merely a "taught programme on the periodical press in Britain 1580-1900." In other words, it is historically rather than practically based.

To gain an overall view of the present situation and intentions for the future, the British Library awarded me a grant to study and report on the teaching of serials work in U.K. schools (and, for comparison, in a small cross-section of foreign ones) and to correlate this information with practitioners' opinions on the adequacy of, and requirements for, future serials librarians. In other words, to throw light on (a) the current thinking in school and library, and (b) the current relevance of teaching to practice.

The Project Plan

Two questionnaires were devised, one aimed at library schools and the other at a cross-section of libraries—public, special, and academic. As the largest collections appear in the latter, so it was to them that the greatest number of questionnaires was sent. As expected, not every school or library returned the questionnaire or completely filled it out. The responses were fewer than expected, but a trend of opinion/attitude was discernible in most cases.

Those sent to *library schools* consisted of eleven questions on:

Staff involvement
How the subject of serials was taught and the time allocated for it
What range of associated academic work was given to students
What short courses were organized, if any
What intentions were evident for inclusion of serials in future syllabi
General comments

Additionally, as the U.K.S.G. (United Kingdom Serials Group) is now one of the major influential voices in the area of serials (not only in the U.K. but elsewhere), some questions were aimed at revealing awareness of its existence and any participation in its functions. This, as a spin-off, would help the U.K.S.G. assess the value of its activities and identify areas for future attention.

Those sent to *libraries* consisted of twenty-three questions on:

Staffing—numbers, salaries, qualifications
Budget allocations
Existence of in-house training courses
Suggestions for future courses
The adequacy of published literature in the field
General comments

A further question on the U.K.S.G. was inserted, seeking awareness of its existence and activities.

Findings of the Questionnaire

Part 1: Schools

Questions 1 through 4 sought information on staffing, courses, parts of the syllabus, and hours. Though a number of respondents failed to answer these questions, it was obvious a wide variety of staff touched on the subject from time to time, in various subject contexts, thus making coordination and continuity difficult to attain. Serials were dealt with at one school only at the p.g. (postgraduate) level, and in another at the u.g. (undergraduate) level, but in the main some form of coverage was given at both.

In the majority of cases, serials appear to some degree in each year of the course, but in one isolated case coverage was *only* given in the final two years. By and large serials were covered within subject bibliography or subject information options, although a wide variety of subjects was cited as including serials coverage, e.g., printing, cataloging, automation.

The question on time allocation failed in its purpose due to the many ways in which it was interpreted. Depending on how serials were integrated into the parent subject, time allocated varied from several hours to several weeks in total per subject *within which* serials appeared. There was no meaningful correlation.

On the question of sufficiency, a majority of respondents thought more time was needed because the courses were too crowded. Generally, foreign practice mirrored that of the U.K. The exception was that there appeared to be coverage in a majority of cases at only the p.g. level, at the expense of other courses.

Question 5 was geared to determine which areas of teaching featured serials coverage. A majority of respondents reported coverage of each area, but seemingly vital areas—history, definition, alternatives, bibliometrics, standardization, printing/publishing, copyright—were left untreated in a minority of schools. One school stated categorically that definition "doesn't need a great deal of time," whereas it is, arguably, a cardinal starting point for any concerted coverage of serials. Broadly speaking, foreign schools revealed the same omissions, although one covered bibliographical and disseminative aspects, rather than organizational ones.

Applications of Practice to Theory

Question 6 sought an indication of the application of practice to theory by attempting to discover whether any visits were made or assigned work given for subsequent assessment by examination. No coordination appeared to exist. And visits, if any, ranged from an overall "viewing" exercise to a deliberate attempt to study one system in detail. Visits of a more practical nature—to subscription agents, for instance—appeared not to be considered. Is the value of visits unappreciated, or does congestion of the timetable preclude time from being allocated for them?

British schools did not appear, to any appreciable extent, to assign work on serials specifically, although they expected the subject to be covered peripherally within other subjects. But in foreign schools, serials work figured more highly, and a majority gave one or more pieces of work in various depths of study.

Question 7 spread the net to continuing education by seeking information on short courses, existing or intended, in-house or elsewhere. A great majority of respondents were completely negative on both counts; only a single in-house exercise was reported.

Since the inception of the U.K.S.G., we have been attempting to promote, amongst other things, a greater overall awareness of the problems associated with serials. One way of doing this is through a short course program, and in this we have had great success. Question 8 aimed to discover an awareness of the U.K.S.G., the extent of the use of its services, and whether the U.K.S.G. and library schools could coordinate their activities in any way. This information would help the U.K.S.G. to pinpoint areas in need of attention. Only one school was a member of U.K.S.G., but a further two did at least seek information about the Group. The member school was aware of all U.K.S.G.'s activities and services (question 9). There were across-the-board negative responses from foreign schools, one volunteering that it thought 'U.K.' in U.K.S.G. implied a membership restriction.

Question 10 sought information on intentions for the future and whether there would be any change in the current situation. Half the U.K. schools, and an equivalent number of foreign ones, reported that changes were being considered. Associated comments revealed a diversity of opinion on how to teach the subject and individual schools' preferences and limitations:

"Hoped to extend *aspects* and develop practical work in handling of serials, evaluation of procedures, and individual research facilities."

"Special option in new BA course, plus integration in others."

"School had education in administration only."

Compare these remarks with that of a foreign school:

We are convinced of the continuing importance of familiarising students with all aspects of serials work. With demand we could offer continuing education courses specialising in aspects of the work.

Others reported that in any course revisions they would continue the teaching as now. One, Drexel University, did have a serials option.

Another preferred to place the onus on students by "following [the] existing pattern, with greater exploitation of periodical literature by students for course work, etc."

The general comments in question 11 were solicited to gain an insight into schools' philosophy, not only of teaching serials but of the teaching of subject options in general. Some remarks were quite enlightening, others contradicted each other. Thus one of the problems of professional education—the lack of standards and the disparity in the coverage of comparative syllabi (perhaps caused by the lack of even a syllabus outline)—was pinpointed.

More than one school commented that serials teaching "must be included in any courses in librarianship but should be pervasive and not isolated." Another went on to assert that library educators are "far too preoccupied by forms of material and really need to address [themselves] to information—it really is not helpful treating monographs and serials as separate entities. This results in blinkering the information search." (The latter assertion is contradictory, for how can an adequate information search be transacted without a sound knowledge of the major sources and their potentials?) And, one said, "it is a mistake to stress format of publication any more than one could help."

Despite the growing importance and growth of serials librarianship and its associated problems, another school claimed that "courses are too generalised to admit serials librarianship. More suitable for short courses." Yet that same school does not offer any serials courses, and indeed indicated no intention of doing so.

On a more optimistic note, yet another library school admitted that "in face of the state of serial files encountered in individual libraries then (if this is typical) there is clearly room for considerable improvement in training." But who is to cajole schools into undertaking this improvement? The diversity of opinion shown here must be reflected in the diversity of training and must, in turn, influence standards of teaching and the levels of qualification ultimately reached by students.

Perhaps a summing up of the unsatisfactory state of affairs can be illustrated by further comments:

"Reliance is placed on students to get some idea via course work."
"Very important for school librarianship"!
"Usually somewhat neglected." [A statement easily said but all too easily *not* acted on because anything else may be presumed to be "rocking the boat."]
"Undoubtedly of great value but mainly to those working in the field."

These comments show a lack of contact with reality; there must be very few practicing librarians who do not have to deal with serials in one way or another.

Finally, one school even said, "It is not our policy to isolate areas of teaching." Yet it announced a new option "on computerized information systems."

These quotations and the survey findings clearly reflect:
(a) variations of local opinion
(b) lack of coordination of professional education in this area (What must it be like in general?)
(c) a failure to recognize the changing importance of areas of librarianship/information work
(d) lack of standards of attainment for students finishing courses

McGarry has stated that "a curriculum must be influenced by, and responsive to, the needs of the environment to be served." Part 2 of the study was aimed at finding out whether or not those needs are being met and how relevant education is to practice.

The Questionnaire: Part II

The general purpose of the questionnaire was to—
(a) find out about staffs, their time in post, and their salaries
(b) find out how they see serials under their control
(c) ascertain the extent of their education for the job

—with the *aim* of:
(a) assessing the current state of education and training
(b) gaining opinions of areas in need of coverage
(c) correlating expressed needs with institutional education

Questions 1-4: Title, Salaries, Budgets

The aim was to determine the range of responsibility for serials supervision and *not* whether there was a serials librarian *per se*. Consequently, the results of the subquestion on salary, though relevant, do not refer specifically to serials.

Not surprisingly, there was no standard job title for the person given responsibility for serials. In two cases in the academic sector, however, a specific post *was* created for a serials librarian, the remainder being assigned additional responsibilities as reflected by their titles—Technical Services Librarian, Sublibrarian/Acquisitions, Assistant Course Resources Officer. In the special library sector, in contrast, only six librarians with responsibility for serials were appointed, the remainder being the Librarian, Deputy, or Assistant, depending on the size and budget of the parent organization.

The overall return rate =	52%	49:94
Individual return rate		
Academic	68%	26:38
Special	48%	15:31 } 85
Public	44%	7:16
Foreign	11%	1: 9 9

(Caution has already been expressed about the figures relating to salary, but they are, nevertheless, of interest.)

Information was requested on four salary ranges—
   £3-5,000
   £5-7,000
   £8-10,000
   Above 10,000
—with the following results:
Total (from academic, special and public libraries)

£3-5,000	0	
£5-7,000	19	41%
£8-10,000	13	28%
Over 10,000	11	24%
No replies	3	7%

Broken down, these figures appear as:

PUBLIC LIBRARIES

3-5,000	0	
5-7,000	3	43%
8-10,000	1	14%
Over 10,000	0	
No reply	3	43%

SPECIAL LIBRARIES

3-5,000	0	
5-7,000	4	29%

8-10,000	6	43%
Over 10,000	3	21%
No reply	1	7%

ACADEMIC LIBRARIES
3-5,000	0	
5-7,000	12	46%
8-10,000	6	23%
Over 10,000	8	31%
No reply	0	

Despite the salary structures raised, a limited amount of credence can be given to these figures because:

(a) On the face of it, marginally higher salaries are paid in special rather than academic libraries. (Perhaps to be expected.)

(b) There are more librarians appointed specifically to serials posts in academic libraries. (Again to be expected. Reflects the importance of serials in the educational process. Nevertheless, there are many large journal collections in both public and special libraries that would, no doubt, benefit from specially appointed staff.)

(c) The comparatively high percentage of staff receiving the top salary was good to see.

Serials Budgets

On *budgets* (question 2) this question appeared, in retrospect, to have been interpreted ambiguously, some libraries treating it as a percentage total of books and some as a percentage total of the complete budget. But, salvaging something and possibly reflecting the importance of serials as a medium for current information dissemination, the average spent on serials in:

special libraries was 58.25 percent
academic libraries was 40.5 percent

In the latter group, nonuniversity libraries and polytechnic libraries reported a significantly smaller percentage for periodicals. The average for the two library types was 49.37 percent. There were no meaningful figures for public libraries.

Question 4 asked simply, "Is your work concerned solely with serials?"

PUBLIC LIBRARIES
100%
0.25%   57%

25-50%
50-75%
75%-
No usable response   43%

SPECIAL LIBRARIES
  100%   6%
  0-25%   6%
  25-50%   31%
  50-75%   31%
  75%   20%
  No usable response   6%

ACADEMIC LIBRARIES
  100%   64%
  0-25%   4%
  25-50%
  50-75%   7%
  75%-   21%
  No usable response   4%

Percentages refer to replies from individual classes and are more mean-ingful than overall results.

The fact that the greatest number of large serial collections are in the academic sector is reflected by the number of full-time posts recorded. It is surprising, however, that a greater percentage of large serial collections is not evident in the special sector, as they are known to exist in the surveyed libraries. This is especially surprising as journals are one of the best sources of up-to-date information, which must be duly disseminated. Here it can be said that the journal 'works' more than the others. In the public library sector, although large collections exist, they are more fragmented and, not surprisingly, the figures reflect a lower priority of journal importance.

Responsibilities of Serials Personnel

A glance at the main areas of responsibility, where listed, is somewhat enlightening on the continuing traditional approaches to serials in the three types of library.

In *public libraries*, for instance, more often than not there was no single staff member having overall responsibility for serials. The position included the normal clerical duties, supervision of newspapers, payment queries, but little fundamental management. Dispersal of stock may play a part in this, where in some cases staff in larger branches have control over their destinies to a large extent.

In *special libraries*, where serials are made to 'work' for their existence, more emphasis was placed on current awareness, circulation, automation, and overall responsibility, thus aiding coordination and continuity. Surprisingly though, few staff were assigned full-time—but there was less fragmentation nevertheless.

In *academic libraries* the management act was to the fore and the traditional custodial welcome evident. Here overall management was assigned to full-time staff in many more cases, but little attention was given to the information function.

Question 5: Professional Education

This question was aimed to discover whether respondents (a) had attended library school, (b) what qualifications they had obtained, and (c) whether serials had been covered, and in what fashion.

In the academic library sector, five respondents had ALA qualifications only, achieved by private study, but the majority had professional qualifications *coupled with* a post-library school degree. Serials were *not* covered in a majority of cases. Some said that coverage *was* given and then qualified their answers by such phrases as 'to a slight extent'!

This situation was reflected in the *special* and *public* sectors, the latter having a preponderance of nondegree staff as respondents. By far the great majority, as before, attended library school. In no case was a staff member without a qualification of some sort, although one had a degree only in a subject other than library science.

To those questions aimed at throwing some light on the ongoing school education program, a fragmentary state of affairs was revealed:

(1) Respondents were asked to state which areas, in their opinion, were given preference in their courses. In descending order of priority, the following subjects emerged: bibliography, abstracting/indexing, cataloging, definition, reference work, automation, journal use, data bases, organization methods, future trends, and relegation.

(2) These were cancelled out by similar areas *not* covered: acquisition methods, selection, management, "all areas" (viz., exploitation, electronics, cataloging, bibliography).

(3) Finally, in an attempt to relate education to practice, respondents were asked to comment on the relevance of taught areas to prac-

tice. The following areas were listed as relevant or useful:
   Knowledge that serials were never straightforward
   Reference work
   Acquaintance with bibliographies
   Use of agents
   None helped!

A few cogent comments are worth noting:

> "I don't think library school taught me much of practical use."
> "None of it was ever mentioned in my course."
> *but*
> "So far as any present work is concerned the course covered most of the
> problems and quirks which I have encountered."

As a corollary (question 6) 21/25 librarians in academic libraries did *not*
actively seek a post with serials, 18/19 in special libraries, and 5/5 in
public libraries. These figures must reflect the position that (a) the large
body of staff who now spend much of their time in serials work (*see*
replies to question 4) must have 'graduated' to their post, perhaps by
default, and (b) in consequence many/most must be self-trained (as has
already been seen) to varying degrees.

It is of interest (question 7) that 45 percent had been in post up to
three years (36 percent in academic libraries, 57 percent in special libraries and 60 percent in public libraries), 12 percent between four to
six years (16;7;0), 16 percent between seven to ten years (5;2;0) and 27
percent for over ten years (28;22;27). There appear then to be no extremes
of service time in any case, but the concentration is within the first and
last categories, with the majority in the one to three years grouping in
each case.

Serials Education and Training

A comparison of returns reflecting individuals' educational experiences
with serials reveals a completely divergent view, thus indicating a lack
of change educationally over all the age groups.

Indeed the returns to question 10, seeking information as to whether
or not previous *education and training* had been experienced, revealed
that the great majority (two-thirds in all three library areas) had had no
previous training in serials work. They agreed, however, that in retrospect it would have helped if they had had some training. To a subques-

tion about *areas* of study that would have helped, replies were so general (acquisition, recording, management, policy, budgeting, general background, etc.) that only an across-the-board education would have satisfied all the expressed needs. Although the question was in part not answered by some, it was noticeable that those who had had *no* training and did *not* think it necessary were mainly from the *older* age bracket.

In all cases (question 11), a simple majority of librarians *did* at least have previous experience before their present position with serials. But this itself varied considerably from being a 'SCONUL' trainee, to work with the British Council, in a polytechnic, special library, or a 'few days.' Broadly, foreign practice reflected this trend.

Work Process

Following the questions on pre/posteducation and training, questions 8, 9 and 12 were geared at discovering something about the work process. The general idea was to discover areas of work with serials that come under the serials librarian's control, whether or not any supporting staff were involved, and which of a series of named literature types were treated as serials.

Turning to areas of work, very *few* had a completely integrated work flow, irrespective of type of library. The following duties were revealed:

Staff supervision	42
Acquisition	38
Binding Automation }	29
Reference	28
Selection Display }	26
Cataloging	22
Current awareness	20

Owing to the inadequate wording of the question, it was difficult to ascertain with any certainty the number of supporting staff *wholely* working in the serials field. But most of the serials librarians had supporting staff, as the following figures show:

1-5	33
5-10	4

Over 10   4

As far as the interpretation of certain named literature types as 'serial' was concerned, the following order of occurrence was established:

Government publications	23
Reports	20
Conference proceedings	19
International documents	
Tertiary publications	15
Standards	12

Individual treatment was also highlighted by those extra categories treated as serial—e.g., virtually any pamphlet, publications of political parties, examination papers, and newspapers.

The problem of definition arose as a result of one reply, which stated that those named in the questionnaire were treated as *series* and journals as *serials.*

Surprisingly staff manuals were more prevalent than expected, especially in the academic sector. They were less prevalent in the special libraries and almost nonexistent in the public libraries. There was an equal division as to their usefulness or adequacy, but their existence was thrown into doubt by related comments like: "No one has time to complete them or keep them up to date."

Further Education

The following questions, 12 to 17, refer to in-house and short or refresher courses, the need for them, and the extent of their existence at present.

In academic libraries twice as many libraries did *not* receive instruction *in-house* on arrival in their posts as did receive it. By comparison, figures were equal in special libraries, not at all in public libraries. Where instruction had been given, in all cases it was done by the previous incumbent of the post or the 'sitting-side-by-side principle.'

Where there was an expressed need for *further education* by far the most popular subjects were: automation (24), updating sessions, new publishing methods (6), management aspects (4), finance, AACR2, bibliographical developments (3), European documentation, and standardization.

There were nearly twice as many (27) who had attended short courses as those who had not (16), and, interestingly enough, the organizations running the courses were: U.K.S.G. (20), LA (8), Aslib (4), BLLD (3), Circle of State Librarians, a Polytechnic, and SCONUL.

Librarians in each type of library were overwhelmingly in agreement that refresher courses were necessary for *professional* staff, and several said they did not mind whether they were held locally or nationally. But taking individual sectors, there was a small majority of *academic* staff who preferred the national venue, whereas an equal division was shown in public and special libraries.

As far as *non*professional staff were concerned, the respondents to the questionnaire revealed that there was an equal division in the three types of library as to whether courses were run or not. Where they *were* held, they constituted a 'general introduction' or 'on-the-job survey.' Once again there was equal division of opinion as to whether such provision was sufficient, although public libraries thought not.

Turning to locations for courses, there was overwhelming opinion that they should be held either in-house or locally. Duration should be one to three days, never longer. On proposed subjects, automation appeared again, together with such general areas as 'overviews,' administration, and bibliographical control.

There are many staff members in this category, and obviously a demand for courses. exists. The problems of allowing clerical staff leave, however, obviously affect day-to-day routine, and this fact may be behind the preference for such courses to be in-house or locally based. By implication, it is considered to be more worthwhile for professional staff to meet nationally, and the necessity of their being away in consequence is accepted to a greater degree than for nonprofessionals.

Serials Information

Questions 18 to 23 aimed to supplement the main body of the survey by asking for other relevant information on the main organizations in the field, the U.K.S.G., the availability of, and intention toward, online services, and opinions as to available literature. In all cases but one (a large city library that had only recently heard of the U.K.S.G.), an awareness of the organization and its services was noted.

On the question of the adequacy or inadequacy of texts, there was general disagreement, some saying they were adequate, some inadequate, some saying too much. A number criticized the American bias of what was available; some stressed the individuality of local practice and doubted its value; some had no time to read. But the following suggestions for further publications were given:

Day-to-day management manual
Handling of microforms
Junior procedural manual
Agents and back-issue dealers
Better *U.K.S.G. Newsletter* or a British *Serials Librarian*
Case studies of British libraries
An 'English' Katz and Gellatly *and* Osborn
Serials and the online catalog

Online Services

The question relating to *online* services was formulated to detect the extent of (1) the introduction of mechanization in this field *and* (2) the need for training and education. The import of the question was, for the most part, lost on respondents. Replies, however, did reveal:
  (1) the extent of mechanization
  (2) systems already in place or under consideration
  (3) attitudes toward the adequacy of preintroductory training.

A majority of libraries (25) reported some form of online service in use, but almost as many (19) said they were not even considering it. A simple majority of the total respondents considered that they were not adequately prepared either on introduction or even to give a considered opinion before introduction, if asked to do so.
  Various data bases—such as PERLINE, DIALOG, Blaise, Dialtech, Swalcap, SDC, Textline, OCLC, Geac, Data Star—were available or under consideration. In addition, several libraries reported their own in-house systems, and others reported that they were 'watching developments.'
  Finally, only a few volunteered general comments, when invited to do so, on involvement in research. Only five said they were involved, but whether or not this could be defined as research is open to question. Eight times this figure said they were not involved.

Conclusions

Many reports compute findings from a comparatively small number of questionnaire responses, and it is surprising how near are the findings to those of the larger follow-up surveys. The fact that these results come from a relatively small number of respondents, therefore, should not detract from its value as a commentary on the state of the art. So:

(1) There is a continuing diversity of opinion, perhaps based on parochial attitudes, as to what constitutes a serial.
(2) Most serials librarians pick up expertise as they go along. Formal education is patchy, as is on-the-job training.
(3) There is a clear demand for short courses, especially in automation.
(4) Throughout there are requests for better education.
(5) It does appear that library schools are, in general, out of step with current needs.

The situation appears to be basically similar outside the U.K.

SERIALS STANDARDS: A BIBLIOGRAPHY

By Charlotta C. Hensley

Official Standards

ISO 3297 (1975)

Groot, Elizabeth H. "Unique Identifiers for Serials." *Serials Librarian* 1 (Fall 1976):51-75.
>An annotated bibliography of articles about codes for uniquely identifying serials, including the CODEN and the ISSN.

Lupton, David Walker. "Tracking the ISSN." *Serials Librarian* 4 (Winter 1979):187-98.
>Describes a two-year study at Colorado State University to determine whether issues of serials had an ISSN printed in or on them. Twenty-five percent did.

Radke, Barbara, and Montgomery, Theresa. "CALLS ISSN Project." *Serials Review* 8 (Summer 1982):65-67.
>Reports on the California Academic Libraries List of Serials (CALLS) project testing ISSNs as matching devices for the consolidation of serials records. Details problems encountered and concludes that usefulness depends on comprehensiveness, accuracy, and unambiguity—conditions not met by CALLS.

"Use of ISSN Encouraged." *RTSD Newsletter* 1 (June 1976):4-5.
>Announces encouragement by the Joint Committee on the Union List of Serials and the ALA/RTSD/SS Executive Committee of libraries' and information services' use of the ISSN in serials data bases. Describes intended uses for the ISSN, including as a "common link between CONSER data base and other serials data files," assignment, and sources for the ISSN.

ANSC Z39.1 (1977)

Paul, Huibert. "Serials: Chaos and Standardization." *Library Resources & Technical Services* 14 (Winter 1970):19-30.
> Argues that the need for standardization by publishers concerning serials titles and the format and arrangement of bibliographic information on serials issues must be pursued vigorously by librarians. Suggests that ANSC Z39.1 (1967): *Periodicals: Format and Arrangement* be enforced by the United States Post Office by linking conformity directly with postal privileges.

ANSC Z39.42

Bales, Kathleen. "The ANSI Standard for Summary Holdings Statements for Serials: The RLIN Implementation." *Serials Review* 6 (October/December 1980):71-73.
> Explains RLIN plans for the implementation of ANSI Z39.42 (1980) for use by the ninety institutions that catalog serials into its data base. In October 1980, only one RLIN member was entering its serials holdings in the ANSI standard field because of the difficulties in using and interpreting the standard.

Bloss, Marjorie E. "The Standard Unfurled: ANSI Z39 SC 42: Holdings Statements at the Summary Level." *Serials Review* 9 (Spring 1983):79-83.
> Details the application of ANSI Z39.42 (1980): *Serials Holdings Statements at the Summary Level* by the Rochester (NY) Regional Research Library Council's Union List of Serials project staff. Summarizes the standard and describes its implementation.

Wittorf, Robert. "ANSI Z39.42 and OCLC." *Serials Review* 6 (April/June 1980):87-94.
> Outlines OCLC's accommodation of the ANSI standard for serials holdings statements at the summary level and describes its implementation in the OCLC Serial Union List system.

Professional Standards, Guidelines, Codes

IFLA ISBD(S)

Edgar, Neal. "ISBD(S): A Descriptive Evaluation." *Title Varies* 4 (July/September/November 1977):33-34.
> Describes the concept, function, and purpose of the first standard edition of the *ISBD(S): International Standard Bibliographic Description for Serials*. Includes a lengthy comparison of the 1977 and 1974 editions.

Livingston, Lawrence G. "International Standard Bibliographic Description for Serials." *Library Resources & Technical Services* 17 (Summer 1973):293-98.

Reviews the development of the ISBD(S) and its implications for the *Anglo-American Cataloging Rules* (AACR).

Rice, Patricia, "ISBD(S): A Review," *Title Varies* 4 (July/September/November 1977):32.

Discusses the ISBD(S) as revised in 1977 to conform to the general ISBD format. Compares the 1974 and 1977 documents.

JSCAA (Revision and AACR2)

"AACR2 and LC." *RTSD Newsletter* 6 (January/February 1981):5-7.

Provides information concerning LC policies for assigning uniform titles to serials, for cataloging microforms, for the level of description for serials, and for LC modification of serials records in the CONSER data base.

Brynteson, Susan. "Change in Rule 6?" *Title Varies* 1 (1 June 1974):21, 23.

Describes proposed revisions of the *Anglo-American Catalog Rules* (AACR), Chapter Six, to result in all serials being cataloged under title as main entry. Shows the relationship of this change to the ISDS and the ISBD(S) in allowing American librarians to use an international standard in developing machine-readable serials data bases.

Byrum, John D., Jr., and Coe, D. Whitney. "AACR as Applied by Research Libraries for Serials Cataloging." *Library Resources & Technical Services* 23 (Spring 1979):139-46.

Covers responses to a 1975 survey of research libraries about their acceptance, application, and assessment of Rule 6 and Chapter 7 of the *Anglo-American Cataloging Rules*, North American text (AACR). Responses show a wide degree of intentional variation from standard.

Call, J. Randolph, and Pearse, Leslie. "OCLC's AACR2 Implementation and Data Base Conversion." *RTSD Newsletter* 5 (November/December 1980): 69-70.

Summarizes OCLC's conversion to AACR2 bibliographic records (January 2, 1981) for form-of-entry differences using machine manipulation of records for names and uniform titles. Projected to affect 13 percent of the headings and 17 percent of the seven million records on the data base.

Cannan, Judith Proctor. "The Impact of International Standardization on the Rules of Entry for Serials." *Library Resources & Technical Services* 19 (Spring 1975):164-69.

Compares the major provisions of the ISDS and the ISBD(S) to the rules of entry in the *Anglo-American Cataloging Rules* (AACR).

———. "Serials Cataloging: Successive Entry." *Library Resources & Technical Services* 17 (Winter 1973):73-81.

Examines the Library of Congress and Cornell University Libraries' decisions to adopt successive entry cataloging for serials to follow the *Anglo-American Cataloging Rules* (AACR).

———. "Serials Cataloging Under AACR2." *RTSD Newsletter* 5 (March/April 1980):19-21.

Reports on the discussions of the ALA/RTSD/SS Committee to Study Serials Cataloging about the application of AACR2. Includes questions arising from the deliberations and answers representing current Library of Congress policies.

———. "Serials Cataloging Under AACR2—Part 2." *RTSD Newsletter* 5 (May/June 1980):29-32.

Relates the discussion of the ALA/RTSD/SS Committee to Study Serials Cataloging concerning the application of AACR2 to serials cataloging. Included are questions that arose in the deliberations and answers that represent current Library of Congress practice.

Carpenter, Michael. "No Special Rules for Entry of Serials." *Library Resources & Technical Services* 19 (Fall 1975):327-32.

Proposes that special rules for serials entry be abolished and that a serial be treated as any other work of corporate or personal authorship.

"Catalog Code Revision." *Title Varies* 2 (March 1975):5, 7.

Points out that proposed changes in the *Anglo-American Cataloging Rules* will be affected by the International Standard Bibliographic Descriptions, the ISSN, the National Serials Data Program (NSDP), and the CONSER project. Raises questions concerning the impact of the proposals on serials records, union lists, catalogs, and other bibliographic tools.

Chan, Lois Mai. "AACR 6 and the Corporate Mystique." *Library Resources & Technical Services* 21 (Winter 1977):58-67.

Suggests a shift from corporate authorship to title as the main element for the identification of serials to bring about compatibility between cataloging rules and international standards for the bibliographic description of serials.

Christ, Ruth et al. "Alternative III." *Title Varies* 2 (September/November 1975):29, 36-41.

Analyzes problems with the alternatives for the choice of main entry in serials cataloging proposed by the Library of Congress. Provides examples to support objections that both are impracticable. Suggests "Alternative III" (entry under corporate body if title is generic or includes the name of the issuing body, its abbreviations, or the title of an official of the body) as the only workable alternative.

Cole, Jim. "AACR2 and ISBD(S): Correspondence or Divergence?" *Serials Review* 8 (Fall 1982):67-69.

Examines Chapters One ("General Rules for Description") and Twelve ("Serials") of Part I of the second edition of the *Anglo-American Cataloging Rules* (AACR2) and describes differences between them and the ISBD(s).

———. "Unique Serial Title Entries." *Serials Review* 7 (October/December 1981):75-77.

Discusses why uniform titles for serials were not required by the first edition of the *Anglo-American Cataloging Rules* and why they are necessary with the second edition. Argues that further development of the concept of a unique title for serials is desirable.

Durance, Cynthia J. "International Serials Cataloguing." *Serials Librarian* 3 (Spring 1979):299-309.

Argues the importance of employing international serials cataloging standards to share machine-readable bibliographic data efficiently. Reports progress in revising the first edition of the *Anglo-American Cataloging Rules* to accommodate ISBD(S) and ISDS and the plans for implementing the new code.

Edgar, Neal. "CCRC Report." *Title Varies* (July 1975):23, 27.

Reports on the recommendation by the American Library Association Resources and Technical Services Division's Catalog Code Revision Committee to the Joint Steering Committee that a new rule for serials entry be written to call for entry of all serial publications under title. Outlines the positions favoring title entry as well as the alternatives. Discusses revisions to Chapter 7 of the *Anglo-American Cataloging Rules* (AACR) and the ISBD(S).

———. "Catalog Code Revision Update." *Title Varies* 3 (September 1976):33, 35.

Announces decisions—made by the American Library Association Resources and Technical Services Division's Catalog Code Revision Committee at its 1976 Annual Conference meetings—of interest to serials librarians. Includes the proposals for Rules One and Six, Chapter Seven, the organization of the code, and the incorporation of this ISBD(S).

———. "Serials Cataloging Up to and Including AACR2." *Serials Librarian* 7 (Summer 1983):25-46.

Reviews serials cataloging before the *Anglo-American Cataloging Rules* and then describes the provisions for serials in the new code.

———. "Serials Entry—Quo Vadis?" *Title Varies* 3 (March 1976):5, 7-9.

Continues discussion of the proposed revisions to the *Anglo-American Cataloging Rules* for serials entry. Points out the problem of writing a universally applicable rule and takes into account all aspects of the International Standard Bibliographic Descriptions, international cooperation, 2nd requirements of automation of bibliographic records. Outlines five alternatives to Rule 6 and the consideration given to them by the American Library Association Resources and Technical Services Division's Catalog Code Revision Committee.

Fasana, Paul. "AACR, ISBD(S), and ISSN: A Comment." *Library Resources & Technical Services* 19 (Fall 1975):333-38.

Opposes a proposal to replace Rule 6 of the *Anglo-American Cataloging Rules*, concerning serials entry, with conventions for the description of serials as outlined in the ISBD(S).

Gorman, Michael. "The Current State of Standardization in the Cataloging of Serials." *Library Resources & Technical Services* 19 (Fall 1975):301-26.

Examines standards for serials cataloging, including the *Anglo-American Cataloging Rules*, the ISBD(S), and the International Serials Data System *Guidelines for ISDS*. Comments on the problem of the lack of standardized bibliographic citations for periodicals.

Hayes, Florence, "Pre-AACR2 Special [*Sic*] Records: Cornell's Experience with a Closed Catalog." *Serials Review* 7 (April/June 1981):85-86.

Notes that AACR2 presents special problems for the cataloging and management of serials collections because it calls for detailed descriptions that will change often. Reports Cornell University Libraries' experience with serials records in a closed card catalog containing only pre-AACR2 records and a second catalog with AACR2 records.

Kovacic, Ellen Siegel. "Serials Cataloging Under AACR2." *RTSD Newsletter* 7 (March/April 1982):22-23.

Outlines discussion of the ALA/RTSD/SS Committee to Study Serials Cataloging concerning the problems serials catalogers experience in applying AACR2. Mentions the numeric, alphabetic, chronological, and other designation areas; publication, distribution, etc., area; physical description area; and works of personal authorship.

———, and Ericson, Randall L. "Serials Cataloging Under AACR2." *RTSD Newsletter* 6 (May/June 1981):32-34.

Reports discussion of three titles, selected to test AACR2 cataloging for serials to determine difficult areas and Library of Congress serials cataloging policies, by the ALA/RTSD/SS Committee to Study Serials Cataloging.

"LC/RTSD AACR2 Institute; Chapters 25 & 26: Uniform Titles, and References." *RTSD Newsletter* 5 (July/August 1980): 46-48.

Includes a description of Library of Congress policy on uniform titles for serials.

McMillen, Carolyn. "AACR Revision." *Title Varies* 1 (1 June 1974):21, 23.

Discusses revisions in Chapters Six and Seven of the *Anglo-American Cataloging Rules* concerning serials in order to conform to the international standards, the ISBD(S), and the ISDS. Points out questions involved for users and library records.

Peregoy, Marjorie. "AACR II and Serials Cataloging." *Serials Librarian* 3 (Fall 1978):15-30.

Sets forth the provisions of AACR2 that affect serials cataloging (choice of entry, statement of responsibility, series statements, and first-issue descriptive cataloging). Summarizes efforts at serials standardization, including the ISSN, the ISBD(S), and the ISDS.

———. "Cataloging Varies." *Title Varies* 3 (November 1976):39, 41.

Points out the impact of AACR2 on serials cataloging. Describes the code, format, the rules governing serials, the use of the International Bibliographic Description formats and punctuation, and the use of the ISSN.

Randall, Barbara L. Nichols. "AACR2 and the New York State Library's CONSER

Project." *Serials Review* 8 (Spring 1982):75-77.

> Describes one of the original ten CONSER participant's adaptation to using AACR2 in its serials records conversion project. Outlines problems encountered.

Sauer, Mary E. "Key Title and Rules for Entry." *Library Resources & Technical Services* 19 (Fall 1975):338-40.

> Outlines discrepancies between the descriptions of serials provided by the *Anglo-American Cataloging Rules* the *Guidelines for ISDS*, and the ISBD(S). Notes areas of compatibility.

Simonton, Wesley. "Serial Cataloging Problems: Rules of Entry and Definition of Title." *Library Resources & Technical Services* 19 (Fall 1975):294-300.

> Identifies alternatives to the *Anglo-American Cataloging Rules* entry for serials rule and the arguments relevant to the concept of authorship for serials. Compares the AACR, the ISDS, and the ISBD(S) definitions of "title" for serials.

Soper, Mary Ellen. "Serials in AACR2: Comments from a Teacher and a Practitioner." *Serials Librarian* 4 (Winter 1979):167-76.

> Details the rules for the description and entry of serials in AACR2 and compares them with those of the earlier edition.

Spalding, C. Sumner. "The Life and Death (?) of Corporate Authorship." *Library Resources & Technical Services* 24 (Summer 1980):195-208.

> Summarizes the development of the concept of corporate authorship and supports the rationale for it. Attributes the abandonment of corporate authorship in AACR2 to attempts to provide satisfactory entry for serials without a special rule.

Stine, Diane. "The Cataloging of Serials in Microform Under AACR II Rules." *Serials Librarian* 5 (Spring 1981):19-23.

> Describes the provisions for cataloging microform serials in AACR2 and points out the difficulties involved.

Turner, Ann. "AACR 2 and Serials." *Serials Librarian* 6 (Fall 1981):27-39.

> Outlines the changes in AACR2 from the AACR and ALA codes, and notes improvements, controversial issues, and cosmetic alterations.

————. "The Effects of AACR2 on Serials Cataloging." *Serials Librarian* 4 (Winter 1979):177-86.

> Discusses the provisions for cataloging serials in AACR2. Describes a University of British Columbia Library Study of its serials holdings to determine whether the choice of main entry would change and whether corporate body entries would be different if cataloged using AACR2.

Government Standards

UNESCO ISDS

Bradley, Isabel. "International Standard Serial Numbers and the International

Serials Data System." *Serials Librarian* 3 (Spring 1979):243-53.
> Reviews the development, organization, and jurisdiction of the ISDS and the operations of ISDS Canada. Covers serials registration procedures, uses and sources of the ISSNs, and the assignment of key-titles by ISDS Canada.

Library of Congress MARC holdings

Hirshon, Arnold. "MARC Format for Holdings and Locations: An Overview." *RTSD Newsletter* 8 (March/April 1983): 25-27.
> Describes the MARC format for representing holdings information in machine-readable form (developed by the Library of Congress and the Southeastern Association of Research Libraries Cooperative Serials Project), which is intended to complement the ANSI standards for serials holdings.

Reid, J. E. Trent. "CANUC Serials Reporting and the Canadian Mini-MARC Serials Holdings Format." *Serials Librarian* 3 (Spring 1979):231-42.
> Reports on the state of the art concerning serials holdings statements and summarizes the *Canadian Mini-MARC Format: Serials*. Appends an outline of the format and examples of holdings statements.

Other Standards

General

Ashford, Daisy. "Serials in Review: 1972." *Library Resources & Technical Services* 17 (Spring 1973): 168-74.
> Includes the National Serials Data Program (NSDP).

Glasby, Dorothy J. "Serials in 1978." *Library Resources & Technical Services* 23 (Summer 1979): 203-12.
> Discusses serials cataloging by AACR2, developments in the NSDP and the CONSER project assignment of the ISSN, the publication of the *ISSN-Key Title Register* (1978), and the use of the ISSN and the *Guidelines for ISDS*.

————. "Serials in 1979." *Library Resources & Technical Services* 24 (Summer 1980):274-82.
> Describes the application of AACR2 by serials catalogers, and developments in the NSDP, the use of the ISSN, the CONSER Project, and in uniformity in union lists of serials projects.

————. "The Year's Work in Serials: 1980." *Library Resources & Technical Services* 25 (July/September 1981):310-18.
> Reviews serials cataloging, the CONSER Project, the ISDS, the NSDP, and mentions progress toward national standards for serials holdings at summary and detailed levels and guidelines for union lists of serials.

Hall, H. W. "Serials '74: A Review." *Library Resources & Technical Services* 19 (Summer 1975):197-205.

  Notes advances in serials cataloging, the CONSER Project, and the ISBD(S).

James, John R. "Developments in Serials: 1977." *Library Resources & Technical Services* 22 (Summer 1978):294-309.

  Sets forth developments in serials cataloging (publication of AACR2), the use of the ISSN, the ISDS, and the CONSER Project.

————. "Serials in 1976." *Library Resources & Technical Services* 21 (Summer 1977):216-31.

  Reports on the progress of the CONSER Project, the ISBD(S), the NSDP, and the development of standards and standards-setting activities, such as the revision of the *Anglo-American Cataloging Rules*, the ISSN, key-titles, and the ISDS.

————. "Serials '75—Review and Trends." *Library Resources & Technical Services* 20 (Summer 1976):259-69.

  Emphasizes standardization in bibliographic control of serials, including revision of the *Anglo-American Cataloging Rules*, the *Guidelines for ISDS*, the ISBD(S), and in projects such as CONSER.

Pound, Mary. "Serials: A Review of 1970." *Library Resources & Technical Services* 15 (Spring 1971):143-49.

  Mentions the National Serials Data System, the National Serials Pilot Project, and the American National Standards Institute's standards for serials numbers and abbreviations of periodical titles.

————. "Serials Interests: 1971." *Library Resources & Technical Services* 16 (Spring 1972):165-72.

  Notes the development of the Library of Congress MARC-Serials format and the assignment of ISSNs to the Bowker data base.

————. "A Serials Synopsis: 1969." *Library Resources & Technical Services* 14 (Spring 1970):231-35.

  Announces the publication of *Serials: A MARC Format* by the Library of Congress in August 1969 as the result of the NSDP, and an Association of Research Libraries pilot project concerning a National Serials System.

Weber, Benita M. "The Year's Work in Serials: 1982." *Library Resources & Technical Services* 27 (July/September 1983):243-58.

  Summarizes activities in serials cataloging, the CONSER Project, the NSDP, the ISDS, national standards development for detailed serials holdings statements, serials claims forms, abbreviation of periodicals titles, and a MARC format for holdings statements.

————. "The Year's Work in Serials: 1981." *Library Resources & Technical Services* 26 (July/September 1982):277-93.

  Describes progress in serials cataloging and union lists, the CONSER Project, the NSDP, the ISSN, the ISDS, the ISBD(S), national standards for summary serials holdings statements, periodical format and arrangement, serials publication patterns, and MARC formats.

Weber, Hans H. "Serials '73—Review and Trends." *Library Resources & Technical Services* 18 (Spring 1974):140-50.

> Includes discussion of proposed changes to Rule 162 B of the *Anglo-American Cataloging Rules*, the NSDP, the ISDS, the ISSN, the proposed International Organization for Standardization standard 3297, the ISBD(S), and the Ad Hoc Discussion Group on Serials Data Bases activities.

Whiffen, Jean. "Introduction by the Workshop Convener." *Serials Librarian* 3 (Spring 1979):221-30.

> Outlines current forces in serials librarianship. Describes the Canadian MARC-S formats, the work of the Canadian Union Catalogue Task Group's Subgroup on Union Lists of Serials and its relationship to the CONSER project.

Holdings

Uluakar, Tamar. "Needed: A National Standard for Machine-Interpretable Representation of Serial Holdings—A Commentary." *RTSD Newsletter* 6 (May/June 1981):34-35.

> Outlines reasons a national standard is needed for the machine-interpretable representation of serials holdings. Comments on ANSC Z39 Subcommittee E's work on a detailed level serials holdings standard.

Initialisms

Sadowski, Frank E., Jr. "Initially, We Need Some Definitions: The Problem of Initialisms in Periodical Titles." *Library Resources & Technical Services* 23 (Fall 1979):365-73.

> Proposes codification and acceptance by librarians of definitions for the terms "title page," "caption," "masthead," and "logo" to alleviate problems that initialisms for abbreviating full periodical titles create.

Serials Data Bases

Anable, Richard. "CONSER: Bibliographic Considerations." *Library Resources & Technical Services* 19 (Fall 1975):341-48.

> Reviews the history of North American serials cataloging conventions and describes existing and proposed international standards as they affect the collection of serials bibliographic data. Describes major differences among these standards and practices and the bibliographic compromises made for the CONSER Project.

Anderson, Sandy E., and Melby, Carol A. "Comparative Analysis of the Quality of OCLC Serials Cataloging Records, as a Function of Contributing CONSER Participant and Field as Utilized by Serials Catalogers at the University of Illinois." *Serials Librarian* 3 (Summer 1979):363-71.

Notes standards of acceptability for serials cataloging from CONSER participants and the Library of Congress.

Baldwin, N. L. Schultz. "BCUC and Serials. . . . " *Serials Librarian* 6 (Fall 1981):41-47.

Reports the work of the British Columbia Union Catalogue Serials Cataloguing Standards Task Group in dealing with serials in the union catalog, including decisions on cataloging standards, serials bibliographic records and serial management information.

Bloss, Marjorie E. "Quality Control: Centralized and De-Centralized Union Lists." *Serials Review* 8 (Fall 1982):89-96.

Summarizes the centralized Rochester (NY) Regional Research Library Council's Union List of Serials project using the OCLC Union Listing system. Describes the approach to producing the list, including data collection, OCLC record selection, quality control for the bibliographic information (the MARC-Serials format and AACR2 with Library of Congress interpretation) and for formatting holdings statements (ANSI Z39.42 [1980]: *Serials Holdings Statements at the Summary Level*).

Bowen, Johanna E. "The Management of Quality Control in a Decentralized Union Listing Project." *Serials Review* 8 (Fall 1982):87-88.

Describes the development of the New York State South Central Research Library Council's regional Union List of Serials project using OCLC. Identifies methods used to ensure conformity to "successive entry, CONSER approved, and LC authenticated" serials records and to using "the ANSI standard" by catalogers in decentralized locations.

Brodie, Nancy. "National Developments in Serials." *Serials Librarian* 6 (Fall 1981):49-57.

Discusses the creation of a Canadian national serials data base and the decisions concerning standards (definition of a serial, the ISSN, the MARC format, holdings statements, library symbols, cataloging data sources) necessary for sharing serials information.

———, and Bruntjen, Scott. "The Pennsylvania Union List of Serials: Initial Development." *Serials Librarian* 5 (Spring 1981):57-64.

Outlines the beginnings of the Pennsylvania Union List project using OCLC, and national standards represented in the *Anglo-American Cataloging Rules*, MARC-Serials, the *CONSER Editing Guide,* and the ANSI *Standard for Summary Holdings Data.*

Carter, Ruth C. "Cataloging Decisions on Pre-AACR2 Serials Records from a Union List Viewpoint." *Serials Review* 7 (April/June 1981):77-78.

Lists considerations taken into account concerning pre-AACR2 records in the Pennsylvania Union List of Serials project using OCLC. All new records adhere to national standards, including AACR2 for choice and form or entry and description. Policies for latest entry and incomplete records are outlined.

Gregor, Dorothy; Tonkery, Dan; and Connan, Shere. "California Title II-C Project." *Serials Review* 6 (January/March 1980):69-70.

Summarizes the University of California-Berkeley, Stanford University, and the University of California-Los Angeles conversion project of serials holdings records to machine-readable forms, using standards "approaching those of the second CONSER edition of the MARC-S editing guide...."

Hartman, Anne-Marie. "Quality Control in a Decentralized Union List Using OCLC." *Serials Review* 8 (Fall 1982):88-89.

Sets forth approaches taken by City University of New York serials librarians to the decentralized production of a union list of serials using the OCLC Union Listing system and methods used to ensure consistent selection of serials entries and use of ANSI Z39.42 (1980): *Serials Holdings Statements at the Summary Level.*

Komorous, Hana. "Union Catalogue of Newspapers in British Columbia Libraries." *Serials Librarian* 3 (Spring 1979):255-79.

Details the history and objectives of the first phase of the British Columbia Newspaper Project, including definitions, cataloging problems, selection of data elements, coding, bibliographic, and holdings formats (Canadian MARC and Mini-MARC Serials formats). Appends the newspaper format outline and ethnic group codes.

Melin, Nancy Jean. "CONSER." *Serials Review* 5 (July/September 1979):99-101.

Reviews the development of the CONSER project from its beginning in 1973. Includes short bibliography.

Rice, Patricia. "CONSER from the Inside." *Title Varies* 3 (May/July 1976):13, 20-22.

Describes CONSER project, participants, development, file format, searching the data base, and the agreed-upon practices and standards for adding information.

Upham, Lois. "Minnesota Union List of Serials." *Serials Librarian* 3 (Spring 1979):289-97.

Presents the background and development of the *Minnesota Union List of Serials* using the MARC-Serials communications format and the *Anglo-American Cataloging Rules'* form of entry. Notes its role as one of three starting files for the CONSER project.

Walbridge, Sharon. "CONSER and OCLC." *Serials Review* 6 (July/September 1980):109-11.

Discusses the CONSER project and its impact on libraries using the OCLC online union catalog. Details the process of authenticating records by the Library of Congress and the National Library of Canada.

Series Authority

Matson, Susan. "Desiderata for a National Series Authority File." *Library Resources & Technical Services* 26 (October/December 1982):331-44.

Examines problems—such as methods for selection, information other than title to be included, heading construction, minor variations in titles—to be resolved before constructing a national online series authority system.

Title Changes

Robertson, Howard W. "What Every Serials Publisher Should Know About Unnecessary Title Changes." *Serials Librarian* 3 (Summer 1979): 417-22.
Points out the costs of serials titles changes for libraries. Lists facts publishers should be aware of before changing the titles of their publications.

CONTRIBUTORS

MARJORIE E. ADAMS is Head of the Continuation Acquisition Division of The Ohio State University Libraries.

LINDA K. BARTLEY is CONSER Operations Coordinator, Library of Congress, and former Head of the National Serials Data Program.

MARJORIE E. BLOSS is Assistant Director of Libraries at the Illinois Institute of Technology.

JOHANNA BOWEN is Serials Librarian at the State University of New York at Cortland.

LEIGH CHATTERTON is Chief Serials Librarian at Boston College.

GEORGENE E. FAWCETT is Head of Acquisitions/Serials at the McGoogan Library of Medicine, University of Nebraska Medical Center, Omaha.

CHARLOTTA C. HENSLEY is Head of the Serials Department at the University of Colorado Libraries, Boulder.

JUDY JOHNSON is Chair of the Serials Division at the University of Nebraska Libraries, Lincoln.

RONALD G. LEACH is Dean of Libraries at Indiana State University.

NANCY JEAN MELIN is President of Melin/Nelson Associates of Mt. Kisco, NY, and editor of *Library Software Review* and *The M300 and PC Report*. She is the organizer and chair of Meckler Communications' Serials, Microforms, and Library Software conferences.

JOHN B. MERRIMAN is Director of Blackwell's Periodicals Division, Oxford, U.K. He is also Chairman of the United Kingdom Serials Group.

CAROLYN MUELLER is Editor of *Serials Review* and Supervisor of the Serials Cataloging Unit at the University of Colorado Libraries, Boulder.

JAMES RETTIG is Head of the Reference Department at the University of

Illinois Library, Chicago, Editor of "Current Reference Books" for the *Wilson Library Bulletin,* and Associate Editor of *Reference Services Review.*
PATRICIA E. SABOSIK is former Director of Marketing for the H. W. Wilson Company.
NORMAN D. STEVENS is University Librarian at the University of Connecticut and Editor of "Our Profession" for the *Wilson Library Bulletin.*
THOMAS T. SURPRENANT is Assistant Professor at the University of Rhode Island Graduate Library School and Editor of "Future Libraries" for the *Wilson Library Bulletin.*
ROBERT S. TANNEHILL, JR., is Library Manager of Chemical Abstracts Service and a member of the American National Standards Committee Z39 Executive Board.
SALLY C. TSENG is Principal Serials Cataloger at the University of California Library, Irvine.
NORMAN VOGT is Head of the Serials Department at Northern Illinois University Library, De Kalb.
WILLIAM J. WILLMERING is Head of the Serial Records Section at the National Library of Medicine.
DAVID P. WOODWORTH is Senior Lecturer, School of Librarianship, Loughborough Technical College, and Associate Lecturer, Loughborough University of Technology. He is also Publications and Education Officer of the United Kingdom Serials Group.